Why Don't Cats Go Bald?

Why Don't Cats Go Bald?

the questions you've always wanted to ask your vet

Dr. Skip Sullivan, DVM, and David Fisher

THE LYONS PRESS
Guilford, Connecticut

An imprint of The Globe Pequot Press

The Lyons Press is an imprint of The Globe Pequot Press.

Cover and Interior photos: Shutterstock.com and Photos.com

Cover design by Diana Nuhn

Text design by Sheryl P. Kober

Library of Congress Cataloging-in-Publication Data is available on file.

ISBN 978-1-59921-233-3

Printed in the United States of America

10 9 8 7 6 5 4 3 2 1

I would like to dedicate this book to Lewis S. Goodman,
the brightest, most generous man I've ever known,
with my appreciation and my admiration.

contents

Introduction

I became a cat veterinarian in Vietnam. I just didn't know it at the time. I had graduated from the University of Pennsylvania in 1966 with a degree in English literature, a considerable amount of debt, and no clear concept of what I intended to do with my life. The United States government helped me make a short-term choice, and by 1969 I was a First Lieutenant in the Marines, commanding a squad in the jungles of Vietnam.

This was a tough group of Marines. We'd been through the muck together, and one day I decided our squad should have a cat. I'd grown up with cats and missed having one around—I had always been amazed by the variety of their personalities, their incredible athleticism, and their absolute and complete cuteness. But more important, I thought it would be good for our morale to have something positive on which to focus. We had a lot of outlets for our anger, frustration, and even fear, but very little for the better parts of us.

It wasn't easy to find a cat in the wartorn, impoverished country. Marines pride themselves as being skillful scroungers, so we paid off a local hamlet chief with surplus goods and he managed to get a kitten. She was as skinny as most Vietnamese cats—and Vietnamese people—and we named her Nguyen thi Meo, which roughly translates to Smitty, the Female Cat. And all these years later it still makes me emotional to remember the impact this little creature had on all of us. We were combat veterans, tough guys, but no cat was ever cared for any better. Nguyen thi Meo made a difference to us. She supplied some humanization in a dehumanizing situation; remembrances of home, affection, tenderness, and a celebration of life. There were near fisticuffs over who would feed her and hold her and just get to pet her after a rough stretch in the bush. We all agreed that as soon as we heard the warning, "Incoming!" the nearest Marine would grab Meo and stick her inside a helmet, then race bent over to the protection of our bunker.

Her fragile, purring body seemed to impart a sense of calm over all of us. She was an important member of our squad. The Marine Corps has a strong rule against keeping pets in a combat zone, and my men became adept at guarding her from the senior officers of our battalion. If we were surprised by an officer she'd disappear inside one of our jackets, but when we had some warning we'd hide her under a helmet or in one of the ubiquitous empty ammo crates. I was taking a chance; if she was discovered we would have to find her a new home, and I could expect a "royal chewing out" that may have ended with a censure or even a transfer.

Nguyen thi Meo grew strong on a steady diet of C-rations and bunker mice and repaid our care with affection and loyalty. As an adult she even protected us with what I assume was her terrific sense of hearing. She would bristle and growl seconds before the incoming siren sounded, which gave us a few vital extra seconds to get underground.

When I was rotated out of the country as a captain I left her with the squad. I learned a year later that she was still doing a good job protecting the other Marines, but eventually I lost contact with her.

Caring for Nguyen thi Meo started me on my path to becoming a vet, but another experience sealed the deal. While I was still in Vietnam, my sergeant, Jess Boone, and I were driving back to Da Nang along Highway One when we were stopped by some villagers. A young girl had been gored in the thigh by a large water buffalo that probably belonged to her family—in Vietnam water buffalos are used for working the rice paddies and crop fields—and she was

rapidly losing blood. We put her in the jeep and raced to a Swedish hospital ship, *The Helgoland,* desperately trying to save her life. She had lost a lot of blood and turned very pale and began to go into shock. I carried her up the gangplank—she weighed almost nothing—and handed her over to the crew. I remembered the way they scowled at me and blocked our passage onto the ship. I'm sure they thought we'd shot her. I learned later that she survived, but it was that incident that made me realize that I wanted to be a healer, not a warrior.

One day, my sister Brenda offered up the idea, "What about becoming a vet? That's the first thing you ever wanted to be." She was right, I had always had a love and fascination for animals, but the difficulties I'd had with science courses made me dismiss the idea. After joining the Marines, however, I learned that I could do anything if I worked hard enough—including pass science courses.

I was accepted at the College of Veterinary Medicine at Cornell University and it was there I learned from a classmate about The Cat Practice, a veterinary practice that specifically treated cats—a radical concept in 1973—in New York's Greenwich Village. I started working there for Dr. Paul Rowan and his wife, Carol Wilbourne, while still in school. It was an amazing place even then: "Patients" were kept in glass-fronted wooden nooks rather than in cages. It was warm and friendly, and shortly after graduating I began working there on a full-time basis. When Dr. Rowan decided to retire, I took over the practice.

It has always seemed to me that luck plays a significant role in shaping our lives, and I'm so lucky to have found this place. I've been at The Cat Practice for more than three decades now. My days have been filled with wondrous creatures that need my help and, believe it or not, some of whom actually seem to understand it and appreciate my ministrations. I've treated thousands of cats for almost every possible problem imaginable—as well as ministering to their owners, who are often upset and anxious and need support. Cat people— fellow cat lovers—are by and large sensitive people who understand and appreciate what I do. During my time at The Cat Practice, I've been asked many of the same questions countless times. What I've tried to do in *Why Don't Cats Go Bald?* is respond to these questions, from "How do I take care of a kitten?" to "When is it time to say goodbye to a beloved family member?" These concerns and more are addressed using the lessons I've learned from my patients.

Chapter 1:

In Search of the
PERFECT Cat

MEOW! **"Some people have cats and go on to lead normal lives."**

—Anonymous

Are you a cat person? If you have a cat, you are by definition a cat person, whether you like it or not. If you're thinking about getting a cat, then you need to know if you could be a cat person. Try this little true or false quiz:

1. You are low-maintenance.
2. You don't trust animals—or people—who'll eat just anything.
3. You don't expect anything to sit, stay, or roll over just because you told it to.
4. A little affection goes a long way with you.
5. You don't mind a little hair on your clothes . . . couch . . . linens . . .
6. You don't mind the occasional hairball.

7. You don't mind shredded draperies.
8. You don't have draperies.
9. You'd rather clean a litter box than take long walks in bad weather.
10. You don't mind sharing your bed.
11. You don't mind sharing your pillow.
12. You don't mind sharing your head.

If you answered true to at least ten of the above twelve questions, then you are, indeed, a cat person. If you didn't, then you might have to settle for—*quelle horreur!*—a dog.

As a vet at The Cat Practice, I've treated countless thousands of cats. As a cat lover, I've owned several dozen, although I use the word *owned* rather loosely. Undoubtedly most cats would consider the concept that they could be owned by anyone or anything amusing. They are independent creatures who some say (dog people mostly) might sum up their relationships with their "owners" as "you scratch my back . . . you scratch my back." That said, cats are nothing if not mysterious. Your cat may be as loyal as a dog, as protective as a mongoose, as wild as a tiger. Cats are much like snowflakes, in that no two are exactly alike.

There are all kinds of cats—and you need to find the right cat for you. As a vet I get a lot of questions about how, when, why, and which cat to bring home for keeps. Often people are looking for very specific traits in a cat, usually based on those things they loved about their previous pets. They want a calm cat, or an affectionate kitty, or a gregarious feline who plays nicely with other animals and/or young children. One client came to me determined to find another cat just like the one she'd recently lost. That cat had loved to sit in front of the television—and the client wanted another cat who would watch television with her. Determining a cat's potential boob-tube interest may not be easy, but there are some answers we vets can give to those in search of the perfect cat.

MEOW! "One must love a cat on its own terms."

—Paul Gray

Cat or Kitten?

Whichever you choose, it's a choice you're going to have to live with for years. The short, safe answer: Choose an adult cat. Adult cats have fully-formed personalities. You know who you're bringing home. But, but . . . I know, I know, those kittens are so adorable. In animal shelters kittens are always adopted first. They've got that whole cuteness factor going for them. And they seem to know that. Who can resist a playful ball of fur who likes to gnaw on your finger with its baby teeth? The problem is that it is very difficult to accurately determine whether or not that precious little guy will grow up to chomp on your fingers with adult teeth. I certainly don't want to talk anyone out of adopting a kitten. But chances are if you adopt a cat at one or two years old, you'll have him for as many years as you'd have one adopted as a kitten. Just remember, an affectionate young adult cat is going to be affectionate its whole life, while an affectionate kitten may end up in love with your expensive couch!

But if you insist . . .

Which Kitten Is the Pick of the Litter?

Many people insist on a kitten, based on the theory that they can mold that kitten into the cat they would like it to be. *Remember: You cannot mold a cat.* Cats do what they want to do. You may be able to motivate a cat (think chicken liver) but never mold one. With that in mind, you must try to determine the character of the kitten before you take it home with you, at least as far as you are able to.

First, observe the way the kitten interacts with the litter. The friskiest kitten initiates play or other activities; she's the one who claims her mother's best nipple first. This kitten will grow up to have a bold, aggressive disposition. She's also the one that's going to wake you up early in the morning by

cat tales: Getting a kitten is always a crapshoot. I raised one of my own cats from about a week old. She was an adorable kitten, never anything but loving and comforting, but over time she went from a calm, malleable kitten to an anxious adult cat. For example, if she was sleeping on my chest and the phone rang, *POW!* She'd gouge my chest with her claws to better enable herself to propel toward the ceiling—to escape from the clutches of the dreaded ringing telephone—and then disappear from sight. Who knew that adorable kitten would grow up to be so afraid of the telephone ring? I mean, who would be calling her?

pulling at your hair. But if you like your cats lively, then she might be the one for you.

If you prefer a quieter companion, look for the loner of the litter. He's the cautious one that always stands aside, watching his littermates play. Odds are he'll grow up to be a more submissive cat than his littermates—and thus perfect for you.

MEOW! **"One cat just leads to another."**

—Ernest Hemingway

How Many Cats Is Too Many Cats?

All of us have heard stories about the local "cat lady"—the half-mad woman in the neighborhood whose home or apartment is overrun with cats. I personally have encountered people with as many as seventy cats. And sometimes more. Such was the situation with a wonderful couple we'll call Mr. and Mrs. Katz. They lived and worked on a college campus, and they couldn't say no to any abandoned, stricken, or desperate cat. For about fifteen years they were my pro bono commitment. The feline population in their home ranged between sixty and one hundred. I was aghast when I looked at their home photos. Every available surface, every couch and shelf, the kitchen counters, sinks, toilet tanks, even the appliances were covered in cat. If this hadn't been a pro bono arrangement, their annual vet bills might have equaled the gross national product of a small European nation. If you can't refuse help to a needy cat you are a great human being, but without significant financial assistance you'll soon be destitute. So how many cats are too many? I hate to generalize, but I think that compassion crosses the line into crazy at more than six. If you have six or fewer cats you're probably okay—but more than six puts you in the same area code as the crazy cat lady.

The answer also depends on your living situation. I'm most familiar with New York City, where a one-bedroom apartment of probably less than seven hundred square feet is quite common. In that situation two cats will fill any extra space. But if you're lucky enough to have a large apartment—the kind of apartment in which you can't stand in the living room and see the rest of it—then go for it. And if you live on a farm and can easily keep and feed numerous cats in the barn, then the maximum number of cats is precisely whatever your spouse tells you it is.

You May Be a Crazy Cat Lady If . . .

1. You have more cats than kids.
2. Your cat food bill exceeds your rent.
3. You go Christmas shopping at PetSmart.
4. You need a king-size bed—and you're single.
5. Your cats have single-handedly solved your neighborhood's rodent problem.
6. Your cats have bigger birthday bashes than you do.
7. People with cat allergies are hospitalized if they walk past your building.
8. Friends think that sweater you're wearing is mohair.
9. You, yourself, are hospitalized for a hairball.
10. Your spare room is Litter Box Central.

11. Your living room is Litter Box Central.
12. What's a litter box?

How Much Does Keeping a Cat Cost?

Maintaining healthy cats can be pricey. In addition to food, cats should have an annual checkup, get the correct inoculations, and be treated by a professional when the situation calls for it. And treating a cat can be expensive. A serious illness or an injury that requires care in an animal hospital for several days can easily cost between two thousand and five thousand dollars. Even basic checkups and vaccinations will cost between $100 and $200. You can see how keeping too many cats can easily put someone on the road to the paw house.

Is One the Loneliest Number?

Single cats can be wonderful pets and there is absolutely nothing wrong with having only one. That said, cats are social animals and they *can* get lonely. I've noticed that single cats can be needy for human attention—especially if they're left alone all day while you're at work. Solitary cats may not get enough exercise—and they may suffer from boredom as well as inactivity. For lack of anything better to do, they'll chase their own shadows, their own tails, and you. And then there's the couch, or the instrument of retribution. Be forewarned: Bored cats may take out their frustrations on your furniture. Or, as it soon will become known, your former couch.

Double the Cats, Double the Fun?

The advantage to keeping two cats is that each of them will remain active when you're not around. They will stimulate each other. They'll get a lot of exercise playing with each other. An added benefit of two cats is mutual grooming—it's very hard for a cat to wash its own ears. Generally they'll lick their wrists and use them to clean their ears, but the rough tongue of another cat is much more efficient than a wet wrist.

The presence of a second cat takes a lot of pressure off you. You (and your furniture, of course) are no longer your cat's sole source of attention, affection, and play. Cats like company. And while it's acceptable and often necessary, leaving any animal for extended periods without company or stimulation isn't ideal. There are some shelters—particularly in large cities—that require potential adopters to take two kittens rather than one. There is a sound reason for this: In Manhattan, many people who live in apartments are gone as long as twelve hours a day. We don't have a rule like that at The Cat Practice because I've always believed a loving home is better than a cage, but we certainly do our best to encourage it. I recommend going for two.

Does the "Go for Two" Recommendation Apply to Kittens as Well?

Keeping kittens in pairs is also good. The ideal solution would be to adopt two littermates, two kittens. Surprisingly, the respective sexes aren't important—but if you do get a male and a female, they should definitely be neutered and spayed—and sooner rather than later. Intact female cats can become impregnated as early as four-and-a-half months old. You can't rely on her intact brother to trouble himself with human taboos on incest. If she goes into heat, he's there. Believe me, they should be altered—and unless you're interested in owning a family, they should be altered while they're very young. Spay as early as four or five months.

It may be easy to judge if your cat is in heat: She will become very vocal, and instead of meowing she will be howling, and howling loudly and continuously.

When petted she will lower her front end and raise up her hind end while cocking her tail base to the side to better expose her vagina.

On the other hand, she may show none of these symptoms and still be in heat. So if there is an intact male cat in your house, or in your neighborhood, or in your country, you should have your female spayed as early as possible.

> **Cat Stat**
> Female cats are capable of giving birth to new litters every four months. At three to seven kittens a litter, you can see why you need to neuter and spay your cats.

How Will My Adult Cat Feel about a New Kitten?

When cats are adopted together as kittens, they are lifetime companions. But if you are adding a companion for an adult cat, it is almost imperative that the second cat you get be younger than six months. Four months old is perfect. The older cat will not perceive a very young cat as a physical threat, and should accept it much more readily than it would an older cat. That said, if you already have an adult animal in the house, you want to find a kitten that will compliment your older cat, rather than provoke it. It isn't really important to match sexes, but it is very important to match personalities. A shy, quiet adult cat may well be overwhelmed by an aggressive kitten. It's important to match personalities if you're attempting to bring together two adult cats as well. That doesn't mean they should have the same personalities—two alpha cats will definitely struggle for dominance—but rather their personalities should complement each other. For example, a bold, outgoing cat will probably

be a poor match with a fearful, retiring cat. Matching personalities successfully obviously requires a little luck, and a lot of attention.

When two cats are introduced to the same environment it's unlikely it will be love at first scent. So you're going to need patience as they adjust to each other. At best, it will take them a few weeks to adjust to each other. So expect hissing, sparring, and conflict. The best thing you can do during this period is stand back. Cats have been doing this for a long time without some long-legged referee flailing around and calling fouls.

Cat Tip: Some shelters will let you become a foster-owner of a cat or kitten or allow you to take it home on approval. If this is offered, take advantage of it. If nobody mentions it, ask about it. This is a tremendous opportunity to see how well-suited the cat is to your environment, the people you live with, and your other pets. For a time we did a lot of adoptions at The Cat Practice. Our policy was that we would take back the animal if it didn't work out. But truthfully, even I was surprised when one of my clients returned a cat—two years later! A few weeks should be more than enough to make a decision.

What Do I Do If I Find an Abandoned Litter of Kittens?

Kittens happen. And usually their mother is much more capable of taking care of them than you are. So the first thing you should do when you find an apparently abandoned litter is make sure these kittens are, in fact, abandoned. This will take some time and effort on your part, but it could make all the difference in their lives. Not to put too much pressure on you, of course. Fortunately, most kittens are born in the warmer months so unless the cats are in imminent danger of freezing to death the best thing to do immediately is absolutely nothing.

Cat Stat

It is universally accepted that once kittens are handled by a human and carry a human's scent, the mother will no longer care for them—and sometimes the universe is wrong. In my experience mothers will care for their kittens after they've been handled by people. Please don't be afraid to handle kittens, however young.

Pregnant cats will build a safe, warm nest, usually in an out-of-the-way place. If you should come upon a nest do not approach it right away, cute as those little critters might be. Mom might simply be out hunting. If possible, retreat a good distance and watch the nest from there. If you have the time and patience, stay there, otherwise you might miss the return visit of the new mother. If there is no sign of the new mother within a few hours then cautiously approach, but stay about five feet away and just take a good look at the brood.

How big are the kittens? If they're mouse-size they were just born. Are their eyes open? If yes, then they're four or five weeks old, or even older. Put down some baby food near the nest. You can buy soft baby food in the market. You might want to start them on solid foods with Baby Food Jr.–brand meat, chicken, turkey, or lamb. This is easy to find and is pure, soft, and easily manageable. Any type of hard food will probably be too difficult for them to eat. If you move away, and the kittens come out and eat the food, they're six weeks or older. This food ploy will also help you determine if Mom is around. If she does show up, you're a good soul, and, most important, you're off the hook.

Can I Really Play Mommy to a Litter of Kittens?

The younger the kittens, the more difficult your job is going to be. If you've waited those hours and the mother hasn't returned, it's time to intervene. *Remember: Protect yourself.* That's right. Protect yourself from those adorable little munchkins because they may bite. Don't take it personally, it's a defensive reaction—but it can still hurt. You might even want to wear gloves. If you do remove the kittens from their nest you should also continue leaving food near it and check back frequently—from a distance—to make sure their mother hasn't come back. If she should return, go ahead and put the kittens back in the nest and see if she'll take over.

What Do Kittens Need?

Like all babies, kittens need warmth and milk. You can build a nice nest box with old towels or clean rags and place it in a warm, safe place, out of the reach of other animals and clumsy people. People will definitely want to pick them up—don't put the temptation in front of them.

How Do I Nurse a Kitty?

Very carefully! To give a kitty milk you're going to need kitten feeding bottles and kitten milk replacement, or KMR, which are available at most pet stores. If necessary you can scrounge up some doll bottles from the nearest small child. Ask nicely. Baby bottles, however, are often much too big for kittens. The KMR should be warmer than room temperature, preferably 90 to 95 degrees. Be patient—it may be difficult for the kittens to figure out how to use a bottle, as it is not as easy as a breast.

Cat Tip: If you can't find kitten milk replacement you can use whole cow's milk. Just add a bit of egg yolk— not egg white. You can also use condensed milk with egg yolk and a bit of corn syrup.

How Often Should I Feed a Kitten?

A kitten needs to be fed every two to four hours. You'll have a hard task in front of you if your kitty's eyes are still closed. If your kitten was abandoned, there's no way of determining how long it has been on its own or what duress it has experienced; so do not blame yourself if it eventually succumbs. Remember that you did your best. I've had to raise many kittens in my career, almost always with the help of a great staff and caring friends—and I haven't always been successful. Even a normal litter born to a healthy female may lose one or more members. Cats have multiple births because the odds are very much against all of them surviving kittenhood. Nature can be tough.

Can I Diaper a Kitten?

Not really . . . but you can wipe it! And since feeding leads to pooping, you just might want to wear gloves. After you nurse the kitten to satiation, wipe its anal region with a warm, moist cotton ball. Both human and feline babies have a gastro-colic reflex, which means that when the stomach fills, the colon—the large intestine—increases its peristalsis. Gently stroke the anal region and place the

kitten in a clean litter box. If it defecates or urinates, wipe its bottom clean and place it back in the nest.

When Do I Feed a Kitten Canned Food?

As soon as you notice the kitten's eyes changing from blue to green or yellow, you should start offering it canned food. That's somewhere between five and eight weeks of age. You can teach them to eat this strange, new food by putting a bit of juice on your finger and allowing them to lick or suck it off. It may take a little time but don't be discouraged. Keep trying and eventually they'll get it.

When Should a Kitty See a Vet for the First Time?

If you can get your abandoned kitten(s) through its first eight weeks, you've pretty much saved its life—except for diseases. Be careful about exposing the kitty to any other pets when it's young. *This means keeping it away from your other pets—even those animals who have had all their shots.*

Cat Stat
Kittens are born with blue eyes. Over the next several weeks, the color changes to its permanent hue.

Take your kitty to your vet for the first vaccination when it's between six and eight weeks old. If possible, bring a fecal sample or two so the veterinarian can identify and treat parasites. Let your vet examine the kitty completely. They might even want to take blood to check for the presence of the

Feline Leukemia Virus or the Feline AIDS Virus (FIV). This will probably need rechecking when the kitten is a bit older just to confirm that it's not simply incubating the virus, and not yet testing positive. Your vet will also check and treat fleas, ear mites, and other maladies.

I Can't Keep an Entire Litter, Can I?

Now comes part two: finding loving homes for your new brood. Kittens should stay together until they're at least twelve weeks old. While they will survive if separated at an earlier age, some very valuable social skills are learned between six and sixteen weeks. You might begin the adoption process by talking to friends and co-workers about how incredibly loving and cute and special your kittens are.

What If I Get Cold Feet on Giving Up the Kittens?

Fair warning: Eventually you'll have to deal with separation anxiety from your brood. After investing all of your time and emotion—and dollars—into the care of these kittens it may be *very* difficult for you to give up any of them. Obviously, it's very hard not to fall in love with a playful fuzzface. But before you make any decisions about keeping one or more of them, give it some real thought. Really take a hard look at your job and your schedule: How much time can you spend at home? Do you travel frequently for business or pleasure? Is there anyone in your environment that is allergic to pets? How will your living situation change in the next five years? Ten years? Cats' average longevity is about fifteen years, so adopting a cat is a long-term commitment. And if you're not careful you can easily become your own local crazy cat lady.

Cat Tip: When you can't keep a kitten, don't be shy when you begin to look for a good home. If necessary, be creative. Tell people your kitty's heartbreaking story: how it managed to survive in the wild after being abandoned by its mother. Try sympathy (it often works). Show them photographs, especially those adorable wide-eyed, open-mouth, and silly shots. Give your kitten socks to play with and take lots of pictures. Let it crawl out of an open drawer and take pictures. People do fall in love with kittens they see first in photographs. There is no such thing as going too far to save a life—not to mention getting the kitten out of your house.

When you've got an entire litter to find homes for, remember to remind possible adoptive parents that the ideal number of cats to have is two—and especially two from the same litter! Let them know that a pair of cats will play with each other, groom each other, sleep together, and comfort each other. Tell them that two cats are no more difficult to take care of than one (cue the nonchalant winks and nudges here), and that they provide companionship for each other when the house is empty.

What about Fostering Cats?

I hesitate to bring up the subject of fostering animals because I'm not sure if this strategy should be described as genius or dishonest. That said, many rescue operations encourage people to take in kittens or stray cats for a few weeks while they search for a permanent home. My experience with clients is that a high percentage of these fostering plans result in permanent adoption. So you might encourage some friends or co-workers to help you out by fostering a kitten for a so-called "brief period" of time.

MEOW! **No matter how much the cats fight, there always seem to be plenty of kittens.**

—Abraham Lincoln

How Can I Tell If My Kitty's Going to a Good Home?

You have made an emotional investment in these animals, so you're going to want to make sure they end up in a safe environment. Before giving away your kittens, unless you know the person or family adopting them, you should check out their home or apartment:

1. Is it clean?
2. Is it chaotic?
3. Are there young children in the house?
4. Are there other animals in the house (and how do they behave)?

5. Does the apartment have window guards or screens?
6. Do the people taking this kitten understand their responsibility?

Really, it's okay to be overly cat-tious when looking for potential parents. After all, these are your kids—uh, kittens. You've raised them to be the cats they are, and like any good parent you need to watch out for their well-being.

Should I Choose a Cat by the Color of Its Coat?

There are some people who pick their animals by the color of their coats. That's ridiculous—unless of course you're talking about cal-ico coats, for which I have always had an affinity. But it's not a good idea to literally pick a cat by color. It's the *personality*, not the color of the coat that makes for a good match. Many people who have had positive experiences with cats of a particular color tend to get other cats of a similar color. For example, many of my clients with gray cats insist that gray cats are the most affectionate cats. In my practice I treat cats of every conceivable color and I've noticed that cats of the same color always have something in common: They are the same color! Other than their color, I haven't seen any remark-able similarities. That said, while it is probably wrong to attribute personality traits to coat color—gray cats being affectionate, black cats being the spawn of the devil—there are some specific physical conditions that *can* be associated with a cat's color.

Are Orange Cats More Prone to Diabetes?

One odd fact that I've seen through my years of practice is that orange male cats that are obese and between six and twelve years of age seem particularly prone to diabetes. But the important word here is *obese,* not orange, because it is well known that obese cats are much more prone to diabetes. And since male cats make up 50 percent of my patients and a sizable percentage of that group is orange, it isn't surprising that many obese older orange cats get diabetes.

Is My Blue-Eyed, White Cat Deaf?

White cats with blue eyes have a tremendously high rate of deafness. This is a fact; it's been well established that this is related to genetics, although the specific mechanism hasn't yet been uncovered.

Can I Tell the Sex of a Cat Just By Looking at It?

There are some people who believe they can guess a cat's sex by its appearance—its conformity, size, coat color, and so on—but unless it's a calico, they're probably going to be wrong.

Is it True That All Calico Cats Are Female?

Calico is defined as fur bearing three distinct coat colors: black or brown (any dark color), white, and orange. This is a sex-linked genetic trait. So the next time you're at someone's house and you see a calico cat, you can appear to be very smart by asking, "How old is *she*?"

When Is a Calico Cat *Not* a Female?

Now, just as there are exceptions to gender rules in human beings, there are exceptions to the all-calicoes-are-female rule. It is estimated that about one of every one hundred thousand calicoes is male. This is because they are intersexes. Instead of being double-X chromosomally, female, or XY, a male, they are XXY and thus male and calico. Fortunately, cats are not excluded from the Olympics because of genetic testing. For an example of XXY—super females—think of the historic East German women's Olympic team.

Male calicoes are so rare that they are prized by the Geishas of Japan as a symbol of good luck and have been known to be valued at tens of thousands of dollars. In terms of size, males are usually about 30 percent larger than females, but that's not much of an indication as altering will reduce this discrepancy. It's very easy to tell a mature lion from a lioness—from a distance, of course—but with house cats it generally isn't possible.

So if you own a male calico you might think of looking at international eBay. PS. I expect the standard 10 percent finder's fee.

When Is a Male Cat a Tomcat?

Unaltered male cats—toms—have significant identifying physical features. There is something known as "tomcat head" (which has absolutely nothing to do with Tom Cruise and Katie Holmes).

The production of testosterone in unaltered male cats causes obvious secondary sex characteristics to develop—the neck and jaw muscles increase in size and make the head look bigger than normal. They look sort of jowly, not in a Michael Moore way, but more like the James Bond villain, the sharks in *Jaws*, or certain NFL offensive linemen. Identifying a tomcat is even easier when the tom is a street cat, because in addition to this he'll have his survival badges—notches in his ears and scratches on his face—from breeding and territorial battles.

cat tales: At vet school at Cornell there was an intersex cat. I think his primary job there was to beleaguer young vet students and knock down their often hyper-egos. A student, not me (any student other than me), would be shown the cat, and knowing that all calicoes are female would promptly identify it as a female. One of my very few petite victories at Cornell took place when I stepped up to the plate and declared firmly, "It's a tomcat, Professor."

"You idiot," he responded gently. "You know all calicoes are female."

"That may be true," I replied, "but I know a no-necked tom when I see one." Rather than offer validation, the profession just asked me tougher questions as I'd ruined his demonstration.

Are Black Cats Really Unlucky?

In sixteenth-century Italy, it was believed that if a black cat lay on the chest of a sick person, that person would die. And although as far back as 1843, Edgar Allan Poe made a black cat the subject of a horror story, some societies—and still today in Asia and parts of Europe—have considered black cats *good* luck. Consider the aged attribute, "Whenever the cat of the house is black; the lasses of lovers shall have no lack."

As far as all the myths surrounding black cats there may well be some logic involved. First of all, it's difficult to see black cats in the dark, which is the cause of many accidents. People have been known to trip over sleeping black cats in the dark. A client told me that when he lived in New York's East Village, he had a small brownstone apartment and in his living room he had a small daybed-couch that he kept covered with a black throw. One night he got up and as he passed through the room he saw two yellow eyes following him, which terrified him and almost caused him to run right into a wall. It turned out this was a building in which people kept their doors open during the day—yes, there are buildings like that in New York—and a neighbor's black cat had walked in and made himself comfortable, becoming almost invisible on the black couch.

Black cats may get a bad rap—but that doesn't mean they're unlucky. I actually have an all-black cat that happens to be very lucky: He lives at The Cat Practice and feasts on catnip all day.

Are Foreign Cats Really *Foreign*?

Ah, mon ami, while I have on occasion witnessed a cat owner berating his or her animal by asking, "What's the matter with you? Don't you understand English?" I have never heard anyone asking his or her cat, "What's the matter? Don't you understand French?" The answer, I absolutely guarantee, will be exactly the same.

So, do Italian cats respond to opera and pizza? Do German cats enjoy a nice, cold beer? Are Japanese cats particularly partial to sushi? My experience has been that cats have universal traits and simply adjust to their environment. No animal proud to call itself a cat will refuse an offered meal of any national cuisine. And it will respond to its caretaker in pretty much whatever language is used.

I've treated cats from all over the world. As my clients are cat lovers, when traveling they often form attachments with stray cats and bring them home. Probably the most common adoptions take place in Rome—I've treated several cats whose former addresses were Italy, Mexico, the Florida Keys, and The Coliseum in Rome. I've never noticed any obvious differences in cats born in other nations. Sadly, they don't even purr with an accent.

What about the Foreign Breeds of Cats?

The easily discernible physical differences are attributable to breed. At one time certain breeds were closely linked to certain locations— a Russian Blue was obviously from Russia—but with easy travel and, let's face it, the loose morals of cats, that changed long ago. A lot of cats can correctly be called Heinz, meaning they have the genes of fifty-seven varieties of cats. We still have Burmese cats, even though Burma doesn't exist anymore—and we haven't started to call those cats Myanmarese. Like every living thing, cats are creatures of the environment in which they are raised. Rather than nationality, it's the circumstances of their early life that most affects their ability to relate to humans.

Can I Adopt a Cat Abroad?

Bringing an adopted cat back to this country is pretty simple. According to the United States Public Health Service, the main issue is that the cat is completely free of any disease that can be communicated to humans. Customs can insist that the cat be examined by a vet at their port of entry, and you'll have to pay for that examination.

MEOW! **"Time spent with cats is never wasted."**

—Colette

Chapter 2:

The Truth ABOUT Cats

MEOW! **"Even the stupidest cat seems to know more than any dog."**

—Eleanor Clark

Are cats smart? Dog lovers will tell you that cats are not as smart as dogs, and offer as proof the fact that cats are impossible to train. But all cat lovers know that cats are far smarter than dogs, and they offer as proof the fact that no self-respecting cat would be stupid enough to fall for that "Sit!" and "Stay!" nonsense.

Consider this comparison of cat and dog smarts:
Dumb Dog
> Dogs drink out of the toilet bowl.

Clever Cat
> Cats can be toilet trained.

Dumb Dog
> Dogs come when you call them.

Clever Cat

    Cats make you come to them. Catch them if you can.

Dumb Dog

    Dogs sit up and beg.

Clever Cat

    Cats purr when you please them.

Dumb Dog

    Dogs chase their tails.

Clever Cat

    Cats chase mice—and
    eliminate them for you.

Dumb Dog

    Dogs need to be walked.

Clever Cat

    Cats walk themselves.

Dumb Dog

    Dogs howl at the moon.
    For no apparent reason.

Clever Cat

    Cats meow at you. And unless you're
    as dumb as a dog, you'll know why.

MEOW! "By and large, people who enjoy teaching animals to roll over will find themselves happier with a dog."

—Barbara Holland

Exactly *How* Smart Are Cats?

The quick answer: as smart as they need to be.

No one who's ever seen a cat open a closet door or turn on a faucet or stalk a mouse can deny that at the very least the feline is a crack problem solver. With its good memory, sensitive hearing, highly developed sense of smell, acute vision, and superior hunting and social skills, the cat boasts a true intelligence. In fact, the cat's brain is much like that of a human—so much so that scientists often study cats to explore how the human brain works.

Most cats are given shelter, food, and love, as well as often-expensive medical care, just for being themselves. If your cat receives all of these amenities, then congratulations—he's one of the smart ones! As far as being able to teach your furry friend how to do things, he may be more trainable than you think—you just need to provide the proper motivation. That is, *you* need to be smarter than your cat.

Can You Really Train a Cat?

The reality is that cats are borderline trainable, but their independent attitude requires that you present any training as a problem to be solved. In fact, problem solving is an area in which cats are especially adept, especially when:

Problem Solved = Food

From a cat's perspective, whenever there is the possibility of food, there is a problem to be solved. That is, how to get the food.

Your cat may figure out how to open cabinets where dry food is stored, for example. My daughter's cats have learned how to open her refrigerator, which has forced her to use a padlock on the door. Some of my clients have successfully taught their cats to use the toilet—and even flush using an electric foot pedal (an accoutrement everyone with

> ## Cat Stat
> In one recent experiment at the University of California at Berkeley, scientists hooked up a computer to a cat's thalamus, which connects to the optic nerve. This gave them a "cat's-eye" view of the world—and helped them better understand how the human brain processes images.

a toilet-trained cat might consider). Other clients report their cats learning how to open house doors, particularly doors with lever handles.

Can My Cat Train *Me*?

Your cat *will* train you—or drive you insane trying to do so. They have the ability to communicate their basic needs and desires—and trust me, communicate it they will. When your cat wants something from you, you'll know it. Cats actually use a form of behavior modification when they are trying to teach something to humans. Typically, they'll just keep getting in your way until they get what they want.

The Cat's Step-by-Step Human Behavior Modification Plan
1. Meow.
2. Rub against something, preferably human.
3. Meow again. Rub again.

4. Knock something over.
5. Knock something else over.
6. Scratch something, preferably human.
7. Bite something, preferably human.
8. Repeat steps 1 through 7 as needed.

As a vet I'm well trained; after all, some twenty to thirty cats a day for almost thirty years have subjected me to behavior modification techniques. Yet even after all that time—and training!—I still sometimes misread a cat's intentions and pay for it by being bitten or scratched. Severe pain—now *that's* some downright negative reinforcement. But that's how cats teach us what we need to know. And we don't forget it.

Can a Cat Smell Smart?

The cat's sense of smell is far superior to ours. That's why they know that there's food behind your kitchen cabinets, when mice are in your attic, and when a dog's lurking around the corner. This is also why your cat may be so fussy about food: Your kitty knows when food has gone bad long before you do. So the next time your cat won't eat that leftover food in the bowl, you'll know why—just chalk it up to its superior sense of smell and swap out the old Fancy Feast for new.

Cat Stat
Researchers believe that as much as 70 percent of a cat's brain is associated with the interpretation of odors, which is certainly very useful when tracking down prey or mates.

> **Cat Tip:** If you want to keep your doors to yourself, use knobs. While cats will get up on their hind legs and try to turn knobs, they fail because their paws simply cannot complete the required maneuvers.

Is a Cat's Sense of Smell Better than a Dog's?

While a cat's sense of smell is far more acute than ours, it falls far short of the dog's olfactory ability. And yet dogs will chow down on most anything—fresh, stale, or stinky. If you think about it, which beast really is the smartest then?

Do Cats Have a Good Memory?

It's hard to accurately assess the depth of a cat's memory. What we think of as memory might just be instinct. Whatever you call it, cats can exhibit remarkable recall. Again, this recall often relates to food. Cats will remember productive hunting areas. People with summer or weekend homes have reported to me that even after almost a year has passed, their cats will immediately return to their favorite spots on these getaways.

Similarly, cats will always remember which neighbors are good for a treat. They will remember those humans who have provided food and/or comfort and avoid or ignore those who have not.

MEOW! **"A cat sees no good reason why it should obey another animal, even if it does stand on two legs."**

—Sarah Thompson

Why Won't My Cat Bring Me My Slippers?

It bears repeating: *Cats are not dogs.*

When a cat brings you something, it's more likely to be a dead mouse than your slippers. Still, like dogs, your cat may very well greet you when you come home—albeit without the slippers. Indeed, if you want your cat to welcome you home, you should capitalize on that superior feline memory by bringing your cat a treat. That's definitely the easiest way to a feline's heart!

Why Do Cats Watch TV?

Many cats (as well as humans!) love a good nature program. For a cat, it's like watching—and hearing—interesting goings-on out the window; they can enjoy the sights and sounds of potential prey but know they can't get to them. It's not as much fun as pouncing on real prey, but hey, it's an entertaining alternative to wind down before a nice nap.

What's Up With Those Pivoting Ears?

Cats have especially keen hearing. Their ears pivot to pick up sounds—like one of those big round antennas picking up signals from outer space—and the large inner surface of their pinnae can concentrate sounds.

They Say Cats Always Land on Their Feet, But How Adaptable Are They, Really?

The ability to adapt to change is, admittedly, another area in which cats receive strong marks. Unquestionably they have evolved into superior animals, at the top of the pyramid of efficient carnivorous predators. But despite that impressive pedigree, on a daily basis cats are most definitely creatures of habit. Cats like a regular schedule with no surprises. Bill Murray's movie *Groundhog Day*, in which the same day repeats over and over again, would be a perfect day for a cat. Bill Murray's movie *Groundhog Day*, in which the same day repeats over and over again, would be a perfect day for a cat. (Ha ha, got you!) Even the slightest change—a new rug, a new roommate, or even a new brand of kitty litter—can flummox them, at least temporarily.

cat tales: This is a story we learned in vet school: A feline naturalist made a blind in a tree for a study in hopes of luring a leopard into camera range. He staked out a goat carcass about twenty-five feet from his perch for bait. Wearing night-vision goggles, the naturalist watched silently as the leopard entered the clearing nearly a hundred yards away and upwind. He soundlessly eased his notebook out of his vest—but apparently not soundlessly enough. As he did so, the leopard froze, flattened, looked directly at him, and, lucky for the naturalist, took off into the jungle.

My advice is that if you're going to move the food bowl, for example, make the process a gradual one. Start to move the bowl to its final destination a little bit more each day. Your cat will thank you for this small act of kindness, and this translates into no scratching or biting.

Cat Stat

We humans hear sounds up to 20,000 Hz, but our feline friends' hearing tops out at about 60,000 Hz. This means that not only can they hear us clomp along, they can also hear the lovely ultrasonic sounds rodents make. More important, their ears can pivot, allowing them not just to hear a sound but to identify where it's coming from—within a remarkable 8 degrees!

Are Cats Divine Beings?

God may be *dog* spelled backwards, as dog lovers often point out, but the cat boasts an equally divine history. Through most of recorded time, cats have held a special place in tradition, folklore, and even religion. Several faiths have held the cat sacred; others have decried the feline as the devil himself.

Why Are Cats So Much More Fascinating Than, Say, Dogs?

Why this age-old fascination with cats? Mystery, elegance, independence, fierceness—all these feline qualities combine to give the cat a mystique that has inspired as much reverence and awe as fear and loathing. Immortalized by poets, prized by farmers, and denounced by popes, cats have held a unique place in human affairs for thousands of years. Alternately worshipped and reviled, the cat has never failed to capture the human's imagination—for better or for worse. Let's take a look at the long legacy of myth, magic, lust, and lore borne by your humble cat.

Cat Stat

There have been many studies that rank mammals in intelligence. Dolphins are always near the top, as are monkeys and great apes. Surprisingly, pigs are apparently quite intelligent, despite the dirty-as-a-pig bad press. In most of these studies, cats score moderately well.

Who Tamed the First Cat?

The Egyptians were the first to domesticate cats. Some five thousand years ago, they figured out that African wildcats were preying on the rodents feeding on their grain — and they began to curry their favor. Eventually these small yellow wildcats with black stripes chose the sweet life at home with humans over the more uncertain existence on their own in the wild. And thus the first house cats were born.

Is Your Cat Really Your Late Aunt Harriet?

Many traditions credit the cat with a special link to the afterworld. In Burma, people believed that monks were reincarnated as Birman cats. In the legend of the Sacred Cat of Burma, a monk sat in meditation before the golden goddess Tsun-Kyan-Kse, who had beautiful blue eyes the color of sapphires. When thieves broke in and murdered the monk, his faithful cat Sinh placed his paws on the monk facing the goddess and absorbed the good monk's soul and the goddess's sapphire eyes. After seven days guarding the monk, Sinh died, and the monk's soul entered Nirvana. From that time on, the monks believed that before they could enter Nirvana, they must spend one last lifetime on earth as a Birman cat.

What's the Connection Between Witches and Cats?

According to the ancient Celts, cats were former humans who'd been transformed into cats as punishment for their wrongdoings. As the Celtic religion gave way to Christianity, the Church denounced the people who continued to practice the old ways as "witches" and their cats as their "familiars."

Why Have Some Cultures Demonized Cats?

Many of the superstitions regarding cats and their fellow animals—dogs, wolves, foxes, etc.—can be attributed to people's fear of rabies.

Rabies has plagued mankind almost since we began walking erect. A generally fatal viral disease that attacks the brain, rabies produces very specific behavioral changes—rage, aggression, excessive salivation, sensitivity to light, and hydrophobia among them. Cats are notoriously hydrophobic—afraid of water. So even though rabies is carried by Canidae—the dog, wolf, and fox family—as well as skunks, bats, and raccoons, it's possible that cats bear the same stigma.

Cat Stat

Superstitions that may have their basis in rabies scares may include:

Bats/Vampires: The victim is bitten by Bela Lugosi and becomes a vicious killer deterred only by bright sunlight and repelled by holy water.

Wolves/Werewolves: The werewolf legend is similar. The victim is attacked by a wolf and becomes a nocturnal killing machine with a very bad case of excessive drooling.

Are Cats Agents of the Devil?

Travel back in time to Europe in the Middle Ages, and the answer could be a resounding yes! This was a time marked by ignorance and superstition gained power. Millions of "witches" were burned at the stake, their cats along with them. Cats were slaughtered by the thousands to rid the land of the minions of the devil himself. The predictable result: a great increase in the rodent population and the scourge of the rodent-borne *bacilli Yersina Pestis* also known as the plague. The pandemic of 1348 and other pandemics decimated the population of Europe.

The price paid for destroying the feline population had a steep economic cost too. Unchecked by cats, the rodent population destroyed much of the annual harvest. On the plus side, the shortage of labor actually increased real wages for serfs and peasants brave enough to work in the fields. Those who survived, of course.

Here's a little quiz to test your knowledge of the cat's unique status throughout the ages.

If a Cat Sneezes, Does It Mean Rain Is Coming?

The hold that cats have on human mythology remains strong today. For example, among the common myths is the belief that when a cat sneezes, we should expect rain. If a cat sneezes three times, its owner is going to get a cold. I tend to think otherwise. I figure if a cat sneezes more than three times, eventually the owner is going to get a bill from the vet.

MIX AND MATCH CAT I.Q. QUIZ:

Match the names with the descriptions.

1. Ceridwen — a. She shape-shifted into a cat.
2. Bast — b. Known in Siam as the rain cloud cat.
3. Birman cats — c. Ancient Egyptian cat goddess.
4. Familiar — d. The Hindu goddess who rides a cat.
5. Diana, Goddess of the Hunt — e. Mohammed's cat.
6. Freya, Valkyrie goddess — f. Believed to be reincarnated Burmese monks.
7. Korat — g. A witch's cat.
8. Meuzza — h. She was attended by white cats.
9. Shasti — i. Her chariot was pulled by two blue cats.

Correct answers: 1. a; 2. h; 3. f, 4. g; 5. c; 6. i; 7. b; 8. e; 9. d

Do Cats Have ESP?

You may think that your cat sometimes knows what you're thinking—or what you're going to do—before you think it or do it. For example, long before you put on your coat to go out, your cat may block the door. Or you may find your cat acting up when you start packing for a trip. Some owners even claim that their cats have warned them that they were about to have a seizure. And I

Cat Stat

Black cats were singled out by Pope Gregory IX in the 1233 papal bull "Vox in Rama." This papal document claimed black cats were agents of the devil—jumpstarting a campaign against cats that lasted for centuries. Some 250 years later in 1484, Pope Innocent VIII ruled that cats must be burned along with the witches who kept them as evil spirits.

can't begin to tell you how many of my clients have told me, smiling, that somehow their furry feline friend knew they had an appointment with the vet and were coming to my office that day, and responded by hiding or otherwise exhibiting unusual behavior—similar to the way children react when they know they're going to the dentist. (I don't take it personally.) I'm certain that there are things an owner does to prepare for that visit that their cat recognizes as a prelude to anxiety, as obvious as taking out the cat carrier or as subtle as collecting a stool sample from the litter box.

Is a Shy Cat a Psychic Cat?

I've had shy cats that would not allow me to pick them up or hold them, but if I happened to fall asleep on the couch watching a baseball game those same cats would feel safe to join me. Certainly lots of cat owners know that their pet refuses to get on the bed at night but is there in the morning—having joined them only after they fell asleep. Whatever the scientific reason behind this behavior, clearly it is true—and just as clearly

cat tales: One of my clients lived in an infamous "haunted" house on West Forty-fourth Street in New York City, a brownstone supposedly inhabited by the ghost of a young woman named Lucy Rutherford since the Civil War. He insisted that when Lucy was around, his cat would suddenly sit straight up and stare at something that wasn't there and hiss. He said there were also certain places in the common areas of the building that the cat would avoid completely because of Lucy.

demonstrates one of the traits that make animals so endearing to so many people. This in no way means shy cats are psychic—it simply means they are smart enough to stay far away from large, clumsy critters.

Can Cats See Dead People?

It often does seem that our cats respond to things in our environment that may be completely invisible and even unknowable to us. One day I was reading on the couch with one of my cats, Renfield. I looked up as the east door to the living room slowly opened and closed. Must be a draft, I thought. Renfield immediately came to full alertness: His tail puffed out and he tracked some invisible movement all across the living room while moaning softly. Just as his gaze reached the west door, it too swung open and then closed.

The hair on the back of my neck stood up—if I had a tail it would have been puffy, too. The house was old and drafty but this was unusual. I began to wonder if Renfield had seen a ghost. It dawned on me that we had actually rented the house after the death of its previous occupant. Naturally I dismissed the thought, except something *had* happened.

Can Cats "See" Other Things That We Don't?

Did Renfield possess some type of ESP that enabled him to sense the presence of the not-so-recently departed? The scientist in me analyzed the incident from every angle. Our human senses are skewed in favor of sight; we depend on our eyes and to some degree our hearing to make sense of our environment, which has reduced the ability of our other senses. Cats' vision is very different from ours: Their ability to see in color is very limited as this skill is just not that important for predatory carnivores. Cats also have very limited close-in vision. They do, however, have excellent night vision due to the reflective tapetum lucidem in their retinas. Their other senses, particularly hearing and smell, have become extremely important and are thus highly developed. They have a far greater ability to use those same senses than we do.

I never discovered what caused the doors in my home to open and close. Perhaps Renfield heard the wind, or maybe he smelled something that disturbed him. And while my scientific training tells me there is a rational explanation for all behavior, I've seen several instances of such behavior that I certainly can't explain.

Are Cats Empathetic?

For all their independence, cats often appear extremely sensitive to our feelings. For example, when things aren't going so well for

cat tales: My cat Renfield was a tough street cat, a survivor. I often felt the only reason he stayed with me was because I could operate the can opener. I always figured that one day he'd decide it was time to move on, and he'd be gone without so much as an "I'm outta here."

At best, Renfield was affectionately challenged. So I was amazed when he exhibited what appeared to be extreme empathy. I had broken three ribs rescuing a beautiful young woman who had fallen out of a boat during a storm. (Okay, that's not true, but the true story is much too embarrassing.) Anyway, I was confined to my bed, swallowing Tylenol when what I really wanted was morphine. As anyone who has ever fractured a rib knows, breathing is a chore, laughing is torture, and sneezing sets up eruptions in your brain of flashing blue lights.

My second day in bed, Renfield did something he had never done before—he hopped up on the bed, smelled me carefully, and then to my great surprise, curled up carefully and comfortably next to my injury. His body did not touch my injury, but he was close enough to radiate his warmth onto the area of the fractures. After initially tensing up, I realized he was being incredibly careful and that he was using his body warmth to help me heal. He stayed in this spot for most of the next two days, leaving only to get food and take care of personal matters. My wife, Ginger, was as incredulous as I was. Renfield usually slept on a rug in the kitchen somewhere within sight of the refrigerator should a stray meal randomly appear.

you, your cat may pay a little more attention to you. One client told me that her cat rarely slept on the bed with her, but after she went through a bad breakup, he took to curling up right on her pillow.

How Does My Cat Know How I'm Feeling?

Many clients have told me that their cat's behavior toward them changed whenever they become sick or injured. In stressful situations, cats do act differently. I can wonder at it, marvel at it, but only speculate about what causes this unusual and unexpected behavior. After I broke my ribs, I think Renfield acted differently toward me partly because I was in obvious pain, but mostly because I smelled a little different than normal.

Can Cats Smell Illness?

Cats have evolved to be able to detect the odor of prey or rivals who are sick or injured. We know for a fact that companion cats in a household will change their behavior toward other cats that are ill. This may take the form of solicitous, caring behavior, or conversely, shunning or even attacking the distressed cat. This happens all the time, and it often takes place days before the sick cat has shown any overt symptoms. I've often said that cats are very good diagnosticians when it comes to other cats and I always ask my clients— particularly those with more than one cat in the house—if there has been any change in the household dynamics. When pressed, they often remember small changes.

Can I Smell My Cat's Illness?

I can smell sickness in cats. It's an important diagnostic tool. For example, kidney disease in cats creates uremia toxicity, which can be smelled on a cat's breath or on its fur from grooming. Also, different bacterial infections may have a unique odor. So we can smell illness but compared to a cat's sense of smell ours is almost nonexistent. It is reasonable to assume that if we can detect the scent of certain select diseases, a cat can probably detect many more odors of sickness.

Cat Tip: So, if your cat's fur suddenly starts smelling funky, you should bring it into the vet for a checkup. Most vets will test for bartinella or take a small gum biopsy to rule out other problems—or recommend a dental cleaning. Cats with failing kidneys get uremic, meaning their blood urea nitrogen (BUN) builds up in their blood, causing depression, loss of appetite, malaise and sometimes uremic stomatitis, an inflammation of the inside of the mouth. This leads to a faintly toxic smell on the breath and sometimes on the coat. It's an odor most vets will recognize.

Certain rare liver diseases can cause ammonia levels to increase in the blood, resulting in the cat emitting an ammonia-like odor. This is one of those odors that I can't smell, but it can be diagnosed or ruled out by blood testing.

Can a Cat Smell Fear?

There really is such a thing as the smell of fear. In stressful conditions, for example, many human beings will perspire—a billion-dollar deodorant industry has been built on the fact that perspiration creates an unpleasant odor. Since cats like predictability in all parts of their lives, that includes the smells of their environments. They will definitely show an interest when the scent of the person who provides food changes. This could mean that they are able to smell fear.

cat tales: In 2007, a cat living in a Rhode Island critical hospice facility made national news. The people at the hospice believed that Oscar was prescient about the impending death of the residents. People living in this facility swear the cat has identified and befriended the next person to die as many as twenty-five consecutive times.

This particular cat, Oscar, was adopted by the staff of this facility as a kitten and apparently is shy and aloof. Still, his habit is to sniff and observe the patients one by one. Then he invariably climbs up on the bed of a terminally ill patient and settles in. In all but one of these incidences, the patient has passed away within four hours. The single exception was a patient who lived twelve hours longer.

Can Cats Predict When People Will Die?

We know that a cat has a highly developed sense of smell. We also know that cats have an amazing ability to diagnose a companion cat's illness: We've seen many behaviors change when a cat senses another cat is ill. A cat will often settle in next to the sick cat and comfort him with licks. Conversely, it may shun or even menace the stricken cat. And as I've written, animals, including cats, demonstrate empathy. They understand on a base level that companions are in trouble and try to aid them.

Cat Stat

Numerous tests and studies prove that the presence of an animal can reduce a patient's blood pressure and induce a relaxed state.

MEOW! **"There are two means of refuge from the miseries of life: music and cats."**

—Albert Schweitzer

Chapter 3:

Living With YOUR Cat

MEOW! **"The cat lives his own life; he expects you to live yours."**

—Nelson A. Crawford

The cat is an inscrutable if charming housemate. In order to live happily with one or more cats, you need to understand what a cat wants—and why. A cat's needs and desires can be fulfilled; you just need to pay attention—and change the kitty litter.

First, you need to learn to speak their language—odds are they can't be bothered to learn yours. The good news is that you can learn to read a cat's body language. The bad news is you may not like what that body is telling you.

Sign: Your cat rubs against your legs when you come home.
Translation: Welcome home. Could you please feed me?

Sign: Your cat meows when you come home.
Translation: You're late. Where's dinner?

Sign: Your cat scratches and bites you when you come home.
Translation: You suck. Feed me now, worthless human.

Cats do "speak" through body language. And you can learn to understand and appreciate that body language—body part by body part.

MEOW! **"My cat speaks sign language with her tail."**

—Robert A. Stern

Can Cats "Speak" With Their Tails?

Tail expression is only a small part of a cat's vocabulary, but it is probably the easiest to comprehend for a new student of Felinese. A cat may signal a change in its attitude by flicking or just bending the tip of its tail. It's a great place to begin your mastery of catspeak.

Tell-Tail Signs On a Cat:
- A tail held slightly straight up indicates energy and a lack of tension.
- A tail raised straight up—completely vertical—and held very high is a greeting to a trusted human or a companion cat.
- A tail raised straight up and held high with the lowering of the chest to the floor with the rear end elevated

indicates that you can pet the cat (and not have to worry about getting swiped!). For an intact female in heat, when accompanied by incessant yowling, this could mean she wants some action. If you stroke her backside and the tail at the base cocks to one side to clear the vaginal area, it definitely means she's in heat.

- A tail that's erect and quivers like a rattlesnake is a conversation stopper—it means the cat is about to mark its territory with urine. Cats spray a small amount of urine, usually on vertical surfaces, to stake out a territory. This is more common in intact male cats.
- Moving the tail sideways and rhythmically—generally a slow movement—can connote mild to moderate agitation.
- When this sideways movement is slow and steady, it generally means the cat is appraising the current situation.
- A bushed-out tail usually means the cat feels threatened or endangered.

Cat Stat
In the wild, cats spray urine on trailside trees at the periphery of their territory to warn off intruders. Domestic cats will also do this if they are under stress—if, say, there is a new cat in the house or even next door.

Do Cats Have Body Language that Admits Fault?

As with most animals, a lowered tail, especially if it disappears under its back legs, is a display of fear and often signals submission. This tail down can also mean "I don't feel well," particularly if accompanied by a lack of appetite, unusual laziness, or hot ears. But an awareness of being at fault or being guilty is not something applicable to cats. Generally, when a cat does something wrong, it's perception is that it is your fault: You left that sandwich on the counter. You put that lamp on the table I walk on.

What If My Cat Has *No* Tail?

There are some tailless cats, but they move their stumps as if they still had tails. Consider it whispering.

Cat Stat
When hunting, cats crouch and stare at their prey—and their tail swishes regularly from side to side, sort of like a metronome. This movement means the cat is really focusing on its task and gearing up for a charge. It's almost as if the tail is winding up the cat for a sudden burst of activity.

Cat Tip: If you do stroke a cat's back and it responds badly to this—running away, hissing, or even taking a swipe at you, etc.—it probably indicates a problem with the anal glands. If those glands become infected or blocked, pain may radiate throughout the cat's entire lumbar area forward of the tail base. This is generally a common, minor problem, but you should tell your vet because if left untreated it can lead to constipation, urinary tract problems, and even abscesses in the area of the rectum.

MEOW! "If cats could talk, they wouldn't."

—Nan Porter

Cat Stat

Researchers in Italy studying the movement of dogs' tails discovered that dogs express happiness by bending their tail to the right; when they are wary or unhappy they bend it to the left. Cats do curl the end of their tail and, while this is simply my own observation, happy cats seem to curl it to their right side.

Can Cats Talk With Their Ears?

Cats do speak with their ears. When a cat's ears are straight up and held alert, it's generally an indication of happiness and awareness. A cat with ears rigid and cupped is happy and ready to play. When its ears are straight out sideways—think Yoda when he was dissatisfied with the efforts of Luke Skywalker—the cat is basically wondering what's going on. Ears down is the defensive position—hold me back, just hold me back. And when the ears are down and held back it's simple: *Now you've done it and I'm going to deal with you.*

What Type of Litter Should I Use and How Much and How Often?

To clump or not to clump, that is the question. Sooner or later, every cat owner begins a long journey in search of the perfect cat litter—a litter that doesn't have to be cleaned out every day, that doesn't smell, and that isn't easily scattered around the kitchen. There are several types of litter on the market, some of them making seemingly impossible odor-free promises—what's a cat lover to do?

Once upon a time there was basically one type of litter, a simple clay litter made by Hartz Mountain and several other manufacturers. But now each time I visit one of the pet-supply superstores, it seems there are more and more litters to pick from, ranging from corn litters to organic litters—each of them promising to swallow odors and remain clumpable for easy cleaning. In actuality, you have more options in litter than you do James Bond movies. Your choice will depend on the number of cats you have, the size of your living space, the medical condition of your cats, and how much you're willing to pay.

Why Won't My Cat Use the Litter Box?

The first question I ask clients who complain that their pets have started defecating out of their litter box is this: "When was the last time you changed the litter?" If you have to stop and think about it, it's been too long. Cats in the wild don't like to defecate or urinate in the same area too often, so whatever litter you buy the most important thing is to keep the litter box clean. It's much better to use a modest amount of litter in the box and change it frequently than fill up the box and change it at longer intervals. If you need an example, think of the difference between your own bathroom and the rest room in an all-night gas station along a country road.

Cat Tip: Cats in the wild use a natural product called *dirt*. Now, the dirt you provide your cat can be sand, clay, hummus, or any of the almost infinite mixtures. If you have access to sand and your cats will use it, you've just saved several hundred dollars a year. However, don't even think of recycling the sand back to the beach. That would be both illegal and really yucky.

Will My Cat Like the New Kitty Litter?

Cats are very sensitive to smells and don't like too many changes in their environment. So if you go ahead and decide to change your litter type, do it just as you would with a change of food. Slowly introduce the new litter type over time so as not to offend your cat's desire for constancy.

The important thing to remember is that you're buying litter for your cat, not for you, so it's best to avoid the heavily scented brands—you may like the smell but chances are your cat will be repelled by it. There is absolutely nothing wrong with the old-fashioned inexpensive clay litters like Johnny Cat. Cats do have a relatively obvious way of letting you know when they're not happy with your choice. They'll refuse to use it, instead choosing to leave reminders of their unhappiness in your path.

What Is "Dusty" Litter—and Why Should I Care?

Many of the cats I treat have chronic respiratory problems, including asthma-bronchitis complex, rhino sinusitis (stuffy nose syndrome), or recurrent tracheitis. For these cats a nondusty litter is imperative and all clumping litters are just flat-out bad. How do you determine if a litter is dusty? You agitate it and see how much dust arises. Basically you imitate your cat furiously digging in the box to bury its business as deeply as possible.

Clumping litter is composed of tiny particles of bentonite which, when wet, will clump together so you can scoop out "mud pies." Unfortunately, these tiny particles can be inhaled deep into the respiratory system and when exposed to fluids can swell up, doing what it does in the litter box in your cat's lungs. There really haven't been any studies about the long-term harm this might potentially do, but it certainly can't feel good. At best, it's benign; at worst it's dangerous, so it might be best to simply avoid clumping litters if your cat has any kind of respiratory problem.

What Kind of Litter Is Best for Cats With Respiratory Problems?

There are several good choices for cats with chronic respiratory problems. Cat Go, for example, is a nondusty litter—unfortunately it consists of wood shavings that are so light and fine that cats tend to track it away from their box, guaranteeing you'll spend more time than ever sweeping and vacuuming. It also tends to hold moisture from urination and will need to be changed frequently.

There are other good choices for dust-free litter, several of them made out of recycled newspaper, often in the form of small-pressed pellets. Litter Luv and Yesterday's News are both fairly nondusty.

Should I Use a Special Kind of Litter If I Have Multiple Cats?

If you have several indoor cats, providing fresh litter can be very expensive, so you might consider shopping at one of the pet warehouses or any of those superstores selling large bags of straight clay litter. At The Cat Practice we use wood pellets that have been designed to be used in self-feeding wood stoves, which are available at large home supply stores as well as any wood stove–fireplace insert retailer. Just make sure you buy hardwood pellets rather than pine. A 40-pound bag will cost as little as $7. Or if you have access to a truck and storage space, you can buy it for only $280 a ton.

Just imagine the expression on the clerk's face when you tell him, "I'd like to buy a ton of cat litter." Believe me, a ton will last you a long time and you can be absolutely certain you won't run out in the middle of the night.

Cat Tip: If you haven't bought a ton of litter, and if you happen to run out of fresh litter and really need it that minute, shredded newspaper makes a very good temporary solution. You can either tear it by hand into strips or utilize the produce of your home shredder. This really is the perfect way to dispose of all that junk mail. I admit I get a bit of pleasure out of knowing all of this wasted paper is finally being put to good use.

Why Do Cats Scratch?

Here is the reality: *Scratching is a necessary action for your cat to keep its nails in good shape and to mark its territory.* You can't eliminate it, but you can channel it.

Can I Train My Cat *Not* to Scratch?

You can teach a new cat new tricks. Sort of. Sometimes. It's worth trying. Young cats or newly adopted kittens can be trained to use a scratching post. But like training any animal to behave properly, it takes time and patience. You need to start with a good post, made of heavy hemp or sessile and that's tall enough for your cat to really *strrrreeeeeeettttttttttch* upward and still not reach the top. Some posts, The Felix Post, for example, have lots of catnip packed inside to attract the cat. Scratching posts are a modern replacement for trailside trees that cats in the wild use to mark their territory, so it makes sense to put them in a spot the cat often passes. Also, a moving toy like a cat dancer—with no small pieces—or even some tightly anchored string might attract a young and playful cat to the post.

Are There Any Alternatives to Scratching Posts?

Pet stores also sell catnip-laced cardboard scratching pads that lay on the floor. These are particularly good for cats who love to rip up the carpet and also serve as good ancillary scratching items.

Some of my clients who live in more rural areas just bring a two-foot section of log inside for their cats and then replace it after it has been destroyed. If you want to do that, with a fire log for example, just make sure the log is stabilized so it can't easily be pushed and injure your animal—or someone who might trip over it.

What's a Claw Cover?

There are products, such as Soft Paws, which are basically hollow plastic sheaths that are glued over a cat's nails. The procedure is initially done by a vet using a special surgical glue, but then he or she will teach you how to replace them when they come off. And they do come off. Some cats gnaw them off or the sheaths fall off as the nail grows or the glue degrades. Claw covers may last as briefly as two weeks or as long as eight weeks. Before reapplying the cover at home, the nail has to be trimmed back, so if your cat is difficult to handle, this probably is not going to be an option.

What Exactly Is Declawing?

Let me begin by describing the procedure: Under anesthesia, a tourniquet is wrapped around the cat's forearm to control bleeding. (Warning: If this description gets to be too much for you, it's okay to skip to the next paragraph.) A sterile guillotine-type nail trimmer is used to cut off the third phalange bone. This is the last articulation at the end of the digit, the "fingertip" that contains the nail. The connection between the third and second phalanx is a mildly S-shaped curve, so unless the surgeon is very careful he can nip part of the second bone or leave part of the amputated bone behind. Both of these errors can cause discomfort even years later.

Are There Any Alternatives to Declawing?

Fortunately, there are now alternatives to declawing, and I am not referring to lead couches. None of these solutions is perfect, but one or more should be discussed with your vet before deciding to alter the normal architecture of your cat's front feet. In addition to Soft Paws and training with a scratching post there is a surgical technique known as tenotomy. In this procedure the tendon that causes the nail to come out of its sheath or housing is severed, preventing the cat from extracting its claws. The nail will continue to grow passively out of the sheath. If the nail grows long enough, it will eventually protrude from the sheath and will need to be trimmed. More than likely cats will endure some mild post-surgical pain—which can be taken care of by painkillers—but no chronic pain issues or damage to the normal architecture of the cats' feet.

Is There Any Reason to Declaw My Cat?

Picture this: Your cat loves to stretch up and claw the arm of your sofa. He's ripped it to shreds, so you bought a fabric cover—but now he pulls that off! You've bought him several scratching posts, but he doesn't show any interest in them. Your spouse wants to have him declawed. The cat doesn't go outside so he won't need his claws for defense, but you've never liked the idea of declawing an animal. It sounds like torture to you. So you clip your cat's nails regularly, trying to keep them as short and blunt as possible, which is vitally important to his health: If he ruins another couch your spouse may kill him.

The most cogent argument for declawing a cat is that if the cat continues to claw the couch—or the owner of that couch—the cat would have to be brought to a shelter which too often can lead to euthanization. I'm positive many vets have faced this quandary and agreed to perform the declawing operation to save the animal's life. I can't criticize or disagree with that decision, but I do wonder if people who value their furniture and rugs more than an animal should have ever adopted that animal.

How Can Declawing Hurt a Cat?

Among the problems can be inflammation at the declaw site or infection caused by poor surgical techniques. But even more important, cats are digigrade walkers, meaning they support their weight on the end of the bone that has been removed. Technically, this is known as walking tippy-toed. Humans and bears are plantigrade walkers, meaning they support their weight on the bottom of their foot. So it really wouldn't bother them to cut off their cla . . . nails. Well, assuming excruciating pain doesn't bother you—that's why pulling out nails is a type of torture. But for an animal designed by nature and eons of evolution to walk on their end digits, the second bone simply wasn't made to support all his weight. My experience has led me to believe that the result of this is often chronic foot pain.

Some, but not all of these problems can be avoided by very careful, time-consuming surgery and reconstruction. However, as wonderful as vets are, like any other business time is money. Especially in surgery—so cost and time conspire to mandate that this type of surgery be done quickly.

What Are the Pros and Cons of Declawing?

All vets are not created equal. In fact, vets are *very* divided about the proper response to this common problem. Basically, there are two very different ways of thinking about this question: What I believe, and what's wrong. The first vet I worked for believed that declawing a cat was an often necessary, completely benign procedure. He told me that none of his "declaws" had ever had problems, but during the brief time I worked for him I learned that was not true. After spending my professional lifetime wrestling this problem—and, unfortunately wrestling cats with claws, I've got the scars to prove that I believe completely cats should not be declawed. So as you read this, please understand it is not an unbiased presentation of the facts.

When I took over The Cat Practice it already was a no-declaw facility, thanks to my mentor and predecessor Dr. Paul Rowan. So all I had to do was continue this policy.

MEOW! "If the claws didn't retract, cats would be like Velcro."

— Bruce Fogle

Cat Tip: Like any type of training, rewards may work. So every time you see your cat using the post, praise him, stroke him, and most important give him something to eat. Conversely, when he approaches the couch or another favorite piece of furniture, shout "No!" to scare him—and then augment that with a shot from a water pistol or a plant mister. Over time this will discourage that behavior and eventually "No" will suffice and you won't have to continue carrying the water pistol.

I've invested the time to train all of my cats—and that includes adults to use a scratching post—and I'd estimate I've been successful probably two-thirds of the time.

My Cat Or My Couch . . . Or My Spouse?

There is no simple or easy answer to this problem. Nails grow. Cats scratch. Fabric tears. But before even considering declawing an animal, think about training, Soft Paws, or tenotomy. If none of those alternatives are successful, and the scratching continues to cause serious and expensive problems, then find your cat—or your spouse—a new, good home.

MEOW! **"After scolding one's cat one looks into its face and is seized by the ugly suspicion that it understood every word. And has filed it for reference."**

—Charlotte Gray

What Do I Do When My Cat Stinks?

Okay, so usually your cat's coat has a little odor, but every once in a while it *really* reeks. You've seen all the cartoons about people who end up in tatters when trying to bathe their cats. So should you try to give him a bath? And if so, are sedatives in order? (For you, right)? My general rule of thumb is this: *Unless you enjoy being scratched, forget about bathing your cat.* Settle for spot washing instead. But if you notice a persistent, unusual odor on your cat, take it to the vet.

Most of the diseases that I can detect by smell, cat owners won't recognize. But on rare occasions cats will emit a real objectionable musky odor. This is usually the result of an anal gland problem and a little spot wash—a careful spot wash—of the hind end with baby shampoo and a thorough warm water rinse will usually clear it up.

How Often Does a Cat Need a Bath?

When my clients ask me how often they should bathe their cats, I always reply, "Only when it is absolutely necessary." And even when you've reached that point, it's probably worth it, whatever the cost, to have a vet or groomer handle it. The reality is that some cats should be sedated before having a bath. That's for their good as well as yours; your hydrophobic cat is not going to understand the purpose of being covered with water, and for the cat it will be a very traumatic event.

cat tales: On a daily basis I spend a considerable amount of my workday with my nose buried in cat fur. That's not for pleasure; believe me, it's not for pleasure. In vet school one professor in particular hammered into us the fact that we had to use all of our senses to understand the problems of our patients. "Gentlemen," he said, "you not only see, you've got to taste and smell as well as feel your patients."

The fact is that odors can be very useful in diagnosing animals. Certain diseases cause very specific odors. So one of the first things I do when examining an animal is take a good whiff. I love the smell of a healthy cat. Okay, call me . . . call me whatever you want. There is a very subtle, soft feline smell that I can't compare to anything else. Cat lovers know it.

How Hard Is It Really to Bathe a Cat Myself?

On the scale of difficulty I think it's easier than bronzing cotton candy but more difficult—and dangerous—than winning the Coney Island hot dog eating contest. Most cats do a wonderful job keeping themselves clean. With all the cats I've owned in my life, it became necessary to bathe them on only a couple of occasions. And those were truly memorable experiences, for my entire family as well as the cat. One cat, Whiz, got sprayed by a skunk. There were two options, send him to the dry cleaners or wash him myself. The memory of trying to explain to a slithering, soapy cat that this would all be for its own good will stay with me as long as the scars will. The other cat had gotten some paint on its coat that had to be soap-gically removed.

Cat Tip: If your cat's coat does smell bad, you should have a vet check it as soon as possible, as it may well be a symptom of a treatable problem. For example, ear infections will create a pus odor or yeasty smell. Most people probably won't even realize this is coming from the cat's ears. Just like in human beings, dental and gum infections create bad breath, which are then transferred to the coat when the cat cleans itself. Oral tumors can also be the cause of bad breath or an unpleasant coat odor.

What about Flea Baths?

Years ago we did have to give cats regular flea baths, but topical solutions like Frontline and Advantage have made that unnecessary. They're safe, they do a good job, and while they can be pricy will still cost considerably less than a destroyed bathroom and a trip to your own doctor for repairs.

MEOW! "I just gave my cat a bath. Now how do I get all this fur off my tongue?"

—Steve Martin

Why Do Cats Have Bad Breath?

Most gum disease is caused by plaque or gingivitis, but there is such a thing as bartinella (it has nothing to do with Bart Simpson). It's actually a bacterium that causes severe gum inflammation in cats and potentially dangerous cat-scratch fever in humans. People bitten or scratched by a cat carrying this bacterium can develop localized swelling and rashes, fever, and an enlargement of the lymph nodes. Fortunately, this disease is rare—or I would get it on a regular basis. Your vet can test your cat for it, and it is treatable by a long course of an antibiotic.

MEOW! "A cat is a lion in a jungle of small bushes."

—Indian Proverb

How Adventurous Are Cats?

Cats generally are wary explorers. Cats explore a new environment very cautiously, often in a circular pattern, gradually expanding the radius from a central safe place. Behaviorists call this exploration *successive approximation*. That's a very impressive way of describing walking around in growing circles.

When cats move into a new house, they'll often stay in one room initially, and only when they begin to feel safe will they start to explore the rest of the house. If allowed to go outside they will stay within a few feet of the house and then quickly rush back in. They will gradually expand their area of security, creeping to the end of the house and slowly widening their circular radii into the world. That's typical; that's the way most cats act.

MEOW! "Most cats, when they are out want to be in, and vice versa, and often simultaneously."
—Louis J. Camuti, DVM

Why Can't You Take a Cat for a Walk?

Sometimes you can. A few of my cats through the years would gladly accompany my wife, Ginger, and I on our family walks through the woods and meadows, and when they did they always seemed to be in a "condition red," suspiciously scanning everything around them for potential danger, for raptors and ambushers. Almost always they stayed very close to us, perhaps believing that since we had mastered the skill of opening a can we probably could defend them from danger if necessary. Actually, that wasn't such a bad idea—there were a few predators capable of catching a cat—including foxes and coyotes.

Should I Let My Cat Go Outside?

If you let your cat outside, make certain it's in the house by dark and don't let it out until after sunrise. There are several nocturnal hunters, including raccoons, that really are dangerous to a cat. In addition, every outdoor cat should have a breakaway collar with a name tag—including your phone number—and also a microchip.

cat tales: There are those brave cats that boldly go wherever they want to go. Whiz was one of the wanderers. He'd go outside and I'd get a call from our neighbor about a half-mile downstream asking me if I was missing a gray and white, skinny, very lovable cat. By the time I picked him up he was as far as a mile away. He was the worst of all types of explorers—he had absolutely no sense of direction. Those people who insist animals will always find their way home never met Whiz. And that's probably because he was walking around outside and got lost. I always assumed he would figure out that if he traveled a mile downstream he would be able to get home by going a mile upstream. It was when I realized that he couldn't figure this out that his name became, simply, Whiz. Nobody ever claimed Whiz was bright, just very cute.

Does My Cat Need a Microchip?

We strongly recommend that all outdoor cats be injected with a microchip. The chips, the size of a lead pencil point, can painlessly be injected under your cat's skin. It's usually done so in the shoulder area on top of the torso behind the neck. Most vets and animal-rescue centers now have electronic scanners that read ID numbers. These numbers are stored in a central registry, which can provide the name of the owner of the cat and pertinent phone numbers. When a cat is found the number is scanned, your name and phone number pops up, and you'll receive a call to pick up your cat.

Do Outdoor Cats Need Special Vaccinations?

Your outdoor cat must have up-to-date vaccinations: These include Feline Leukemia, a Distemper-Pneumonia combo shot, and most especially one for rabies. New York is among several states that require rabies vaccinations for all cats and dogs, whether they are indoor or outdoor animals. The primary animals that carry rabies are members of the canine family. I live in Connecticut and fully 50 percent of our resident raccoons tested positive for rabies in 2006. Rabies is a horrible disease, it's a killer, and every responsible pet owner needs to take positive steps to protect their pets and family from infection.

Skunks and bats also carry rabies. Unfortunately, many cats are curious enough or aggressive enough to mess with either of these nocturnal creatures. For that reason cats have to be inoculated. Not only does their health depend on it, yours does too.

What Do I Do When My Cat Won't Chase Mice?

Not all cats chase mice. So if you have a pest problem, you'll need to keep the safety of that cat in mind when you choose a way to get rid of the mice. Local hardware stores, Lowes, or Home Depot offer a variety of pest traps. Among the safest for your animals are the small Have A Heart traps that catch rodents without injuring them. These are perfect for those among us who just can't bring ourselves to kill living creatures. Of course, the real test of your morality comes after you've caught a mouse and have to decide what to do with it. And then you think about that neighbor two doors down who yelled at your kid and . . .

Cat Tip: Beware: Bats are very attractive to cats. Why not? A bat is basically a bird-mouse, so obviously it's a cat magnet. Bats are also known to come to cats—flying into houses and even apartments and getting trapped there. That's one reason indoor cats need to have their rabies shots too.

Are Glue Traps Safe?

Common glue traps are also quite safe for cats. Cats generally will avoid them, but even if they make a mistake and step on one, the glue just isn't strong enough to hold or injure a 7- to 20-pound cat. The mouse is a different story though. Mice will get trapped and starve or break bones as it struggles to get free and you might cripple it when you try to liberate it outdoors—if that's your intention. If you do, by the way, make sure you wear gloves, as a desperate mouse or rat will bite.

> **Cat Tip:** Sonic devices are probably safe for cats. These plug-in devices broadcast ultrahigh-frequency sounds that supposedly drive mice away. Some people swear by them. But if your cat seems agitated near these devices or avoids the rooms in which they are being used, you can be certain the sounds are bothering your cat.

Are Spring Traps Really Dangerous?

Regular spring-driven mousetraps that you bait with cheese or peanut butter are not safe for cats. Cats can easily injure their paws or noses trying to get the food; and while the injuries are almost always minor they should be avoided. The only place I would advise using these snap traps are in small spaces not easily reached by cats, like inside cabinets.

cat tales: I had a patient who patrolled the basement of a large apartment building. Unknown to that pet's owner, the super-intendent used D-Con bait throughout the basement. The cat was brought to the Practice because his owner couldn't stop the bleeding from a small cut on its forearm. It should have been a meaningless wound, but we couldn't stop the bleeding. We tried everything from pressure dressings to temporary tourniquets without success. While the bleeding was not heavy, it was dog-gedly persistent. The cat was growing more anemic by the hour. We had to do something or the cat was going to die.

I took a guess. Since the wound looked like it might be a rodent bite I told the owner to call the building's super and ask if he used rodenticides in the building. When I found out he used D-Con, I knew what the problem was. We injected clotting factors into the cat and the bleeding stopped within minutes.

Are Poison Traps Ever Safe?

Never use poison traps. Poison baits are not safe for cats. While most cats will not be interested in the bait, these traps still should not be used in a home with a cat. The serious problem is that these baits kill mice by poisoning them with an anticlotting substance. Cats that eat enough of these poisoned rodents can actually suffer the same consequences—poor or no clotting, which is also known as feline hemophilia.

Should I Use a Professional Exterminator?

Professional exterminators are the great unknown. They need to be advised that there are cats in the environment and asked if the chemicals they are using are safe for larger animals. Double-check them by getting the scientific name of the substance and calling poison control—your vet will give you the number—to determine if it is really safe. There may be a small charge, but it is nothing compared to the value of your pet's life.

MEOW! **"It is better to feed one cat than many mice."**

—Norwegian proverb

Chapter 4:

Health AND FITness

MEOW! **"Cats are rather delicate creatures and they are subject to a lot of ailments, but I never heard of one who suffered from insomnia."**

—Joseph Wood Crutch

A healthy, fit cat is a happy cat. However, given that the cat's most preferred activities are sleeping and eating, and its least preferred activities are trips to the vet, you may wonder how you can keep a cat happy and fit. First, let's examine the cat's typical daily health and fitness routine:

12 a.m.: Midnight Snack
12:30 to 6 a.m.: Bedtime on human's pillow
6 to 6:30 a.m.: Tap human's head until awake
6:30 to 7 a.m.: Eat Breakfast
7 a.m. to 12 p.m.: Morning nap on padded kitchen chair
12 p.m.: Lunch
12:30 to 3 p.m.: Siesta in afternoon sun

Why Don't Cats Go Bald?

3 p.m.: Cream and catnip break
3:30 to 6 p.m.: Power nap on couch
6:30 p.m.: Dinner
7 to 9 p.m.: Play with human
9 p.m. to 12 a.m.: Doze on human's lap

This strenuous feline routine puts the onus on us humans to ensure that our cats remain fit and healthy. Let's take a look at the ways in which we can help ensure their continued well-being—without getting scratched!

Can I Medicate My Cat Without Going to the Vet?

Let's start with a warning: Cats have unique metabolic pathways in their livers that make some drugs that are extremely safe in people, and even in dogs, dangerous or deadly in cats. This is why most feline practitioners spend a good deal of their time cautioning clients to avoid home remedies. That said, a few of the meds in your bathroom cabinet will work with cats—but only a few. As a general rule, unless you have specific approval from a knowledgeable source, don't give your cat any of your own medications. Usually the result will not be what you intend it to be.

Can I Give My Ailing Cat an Aspirin?

Should you give your cat an aspirin or any other non-steroidal anti-inflammatory drugs? Maybe. In very small amounts, aspirin can be very useful. If your healthy cat should get stung by a bee on its nose or paw or tear a nail, it's fine to treat it with one-quarter of a bufferin or a whole buffered baby aspirin. Aspirin can also help older, arthritic cats both with the inflammation and pain associated with arthritis and other joint problems. But the amount of aspirin given to a cat is critical. An average-size cat should receive no more than one 5-grain aspirin tablet per *week*! The usual dose I prescribe is one-quarter of a buffered aspirin Monday, Wednesday, and Saturday. There are some cats that just don't tolerate aspirin, even buffered aspirin. It can produce a lack of appetite, vomiting, and diarrhea. These symptoms will be obvious, and if they occur stop giving your cat whatever drug is bothering him and find an alternative.

Fortunately, that's unusual, as most cats tolerate aspirin well. As in humans, in addition to its use as an anti-inflammatory drug, aspirin is useful in anticoagulation therapy in cats with heart disease. Many cats with heart problems suffer from dilation—enlargement—of the upper chambers of their hearts. The blood flow in these ballooned out compartments can become stagnant, allowing potentially deadly clots to form. If these clots are pumped back into a cardiac artery, this can cause the classic myocardial infarction—a heart attack. In cats, a common result of heart disease with atrial enlargement can lead to a clot forming that is pumped down the aorta to the point at which it divides into the two major femoral arteries. This is the main blood supply to the animal's hind legs. This is called a "saddle emboli," as it blocks the blood flow to the rear legs. Aspirin therapy helps prevent this very painful and often untreatable disease from occurring.

Are There Other Arthritis Remedies for My Cat?

Glucosamine Chondroitin Sulfate is used by many people to treat arthritis and other joint problems—and will have no negative effect on a cat. However, there are many antiarthritic drugs prescribed for humans that are dangerous to cats.

Can I Give My Cat Other "People" Pain Killers?

Never, ever, ever, ever give Excedrin, Aleve, Advil, or any similar products to your cat. Drugs that contain naproxen or ibuprofen, which are completely harmless at the correct dosage in human beings have proved to be fatal to a cat. A cat's liver just isn't capable of processing these drugs.

But some common older antibiotics are marginally acceptable. Let's take an example: Two of the most common antibiotics are penicillin and streptomycin. Penicillin is extremely safe in cats, and we can give huge amounts of it in treatment with absolutely no problem. Conversely, streptomycin in even modest amounts can cause severe toxicity in cats—which can result in a range of problems from kidney damage to deafness caused by the destruction of the inner and middle ear components.

It bears repeating: *Never give a cat any drug containing naproxen, ibuprofen or acetaminophen.* In addition, the most commonly dispensed painkillers, Percodan and Percoset, contain the prohibited NSAIDS, so don't be tempted to give any of those painkillers to your cat. Additionally, hydrocodone is not good for cats.

What Do I Do When My Cat Has a Skin Problem?

Cats can and do get a bewildering variety of dermatological problems. For minor rashes, bug bites, and minor skin irritations, aloe is completely safe. But you might also try the sap from the jewelweed plant, which is safe and very soothing. This is a wetland plant that grows around ponds. If you're unfamiliar with it, ask a gardener or look on the Internet. Vitamin E oil rubbed into the wound is safe in small amounts and can be very helpful in promoting healing; this is especially useful when your cat's nose gets irritated from the constant licking of a dripping nose caused by a feline upper respiratory infection. Cats tend to lick off anything on their fur or skin, so use only a small amount.

Because cats will ingest whatever you put on their coat, you need to know the makeup of any ointment you use. The most common antibiotic skin preparations for human beings contain neomycin, polymixin and bacitraccin. These are all safe if used in small amounts and rubbed in like a vanishing cream. Other skin medications for humans may well contain cortisone. Over-the-counter preparations of cortisone are usually 0.5 percent to 1 percent hydrocortisone. And these products are also safe if rubbed in well.

> **Cat Tip:** If your cat's skin problem lasts more than a few days, you should consult your vet. It will be very difficult for you to determine from the appearance of the rash or eruption whether it is bacterial, fungal, parasitic, or inflammatory, and they can require different treatment.

How Do I Treat My Cat's Tummy Ache?

Cats vomit. But you probably already know that. In fact, I'm *sure* you know that. Pepcid AC, 10 mg, is an over-the-counter drug that reduces stomach acid. This is very safe for cats. The dosage should be one-quarter tab twice per day in small and medium-size cats and one-half of a tablet twice per day in larger cats. But vomiting for more than twenty-four hours requires the attention of your vet.

What Can I Do about My Cat's Diarrhea—Fast?

It happens. And it actually can be a symptom of many things. But it also can be caused by a bad stomach. We used to use Kaopectate as a benign diarrhea treatment, but it now contains aspirin—as does Pepto-Bismol—so it should be avoided. Because the size of the dose may vary, it's impossible to determine the amount of aspirin in each dose, so the potential for an overdose is very real. Ask your druggist if he has a mixture of kaolin and pectin without aspirin; that's what you want to use for the first twenty-four hours. We also recommend a mixture of finely chopped fresh turkey or baby food meat turkey mixed 50-50 with very well cooked brown rice. Both of these are mildly constipating and may successfully arrest a mild, transient diarrhea episode.

What Can I Do about My Cat's Constipation—Fast?

There are a lot of ways to treat constipation. Many hairball products like Laxaire, Petromalt, and Laxatone can be helpful in treating mild constipation. So can Metamucil and psyllium seeds. But severe or chronically hard stools and straining can be a symptom of a serious problem—and one you shouldn't try to treat yourself. A vet can suggest appropriate changes in diet or the proper medication to ease bowel movements. Constipation should be treated aggressively as it is progressive. Each episode can stretch and weaken the colon and over time it can evolve into obstipation, which is serious constipation requiring enemas, or manual evacuation of the colon under anesthesia.

How Should I Give My Cat an Enema?

Very carefully! Believe it or not there are pet enemas that are available at pet stores. This is recommended only for mild, transient hard stools. And truthfully, not only is this difficult to do in many cats, but if it should work . . . well, let's just say that the result may not be so pleasant. Most cats won't be able to control their subsequent movements—meaning bad things will happen to your furnishings.

MEOW! **"Even overweight, cats instinctively know the cardinal rule: when fat, arrange yourself in slim poses."**

—John Weitz

Why Are Cats So Prone to Diabetes?

Unfortunately, diabetes is very common in domestic cats. This is probably because they eat too much and get too little exercise. They spend much of the day agitating for food, often until you are forced to make a Neville Chamberlain "peace at any price" decision.

cat tales: Diabetes in cats is markedly different than diabetes in human beings. People can develop severe secondary problems, including blindness and visual impairment and severe circulatory problems. Fortunately, if cats are even moderately well regulated they escape these consequences. But it is critical that you work with your vet to make sure your cat is well regulated. My own cat, Renfield, became diabetic when he was only eight years old, but with regular insulin injections, attention to diet, and careful monitoring he lived happily another ten years. So the good news is that a diabetic cat can have a good quality of life if you take good care.

Cats generally require only a small amount of insulin, between one to six units twice a day, so the cost is not prohibitive. We also recommend very fine insulin needles that the cat won't even feel. Remember, cats don't have very many pain sensors in their skin, so they won't feel the daily insulin injections or even the tiny ear prick necessary to get a drop of blood for blood glucose testing.

We used to do things a little different. In the old days I measured Renfield's needs for insulin with periodic urine glucose tests, but the blood monitoring available currently is easier and more accurate.

What Are the Signs of Diabetes?

If you notice your cat drinking more water than usual and urinating in large amounts you should have him examined by your vet. Especially if he is overweight and has large dandruff flakes on his lower back. Don't delay: Unidentified and untreated diabetes will usually lead to significant liver problems within a few months. The diabetes causes the formation of ketones—toxic substances like acetone—which can be fatal.

How Do I Treat My Diabetic Cat?

Treating a diabetic cat is a labor of love, but it is hard work. The cat is probably going to need two injections of insulin a day and someone is going to have to monitor his blood or urine sugar levels. The cat will also need a special diet to help it lose weight. Attention to the amount and timing of the feeding is important, as almost one-third of all the cats I treat can recover from diabetes and then no longer need insulin shots. But the key is that they need to lose their excess weight slowly.

Cat Tip: Your vet can perform simple tests to determine if your cat is diabetic. For a vet, diabetes is relatively easy to treat if we get the complete cooperation of the pet's owner, and cats respond extremely well to that treatment. It bought Renfield an extra ten years of life—and you can do the same thing for your cat.

Why Does My Cat Vomit So Often?

The cat's tendency to vomit is legendary. Sometimes the reason becomes obvious: a hairball, grass, or the occasional rodent part. Don't worry, it's a common problem. Many of my clients describe their cats as "powerpukers." Even comic cats like *Garfield* are portrayed as constantly throwing up hairballs. In fact, it usually is the best way to get guests who stay too late to decide it's time to depart.

When Is a Hairball Really a Hairball?

Cats do often vomit hairballs. That said, this is a common subject that is often misunderstood by cat lovers and cat haters alike. When a cat vomits, there is likely to be a significant amount of hair in the vomitus, as they are constantly ingesting it during their grooming activity. These loose amounts of hair don't qualify as hairballs. But when your cat pukes up a hard, tubular mass of hair—that's a hairball.

Why Do Cats Vomit So Many Hairballs?

Hairballs are natural. When the amount of hair in the stomach builds and forms a hairball, there are only two ways your cat may expel it: vomiting it up or passing it through the intestine. Most hairballs are actually expelled this latter way, which is why we often find hairballs in the litter box covered with a glaze of fecal material. We often see stools that look normal but when we dissect them, as much as 80 percent of the stool might be concretized hair, a hairball that passed through the colon.

Do Cats *Cough* Up Hairballs?

This is probably the question I am asked most often by my clients. A cat's cough can generally be distinguished by its hacking or honking sound. You should be aware of the causes, but many causes of a cough can easily be treated. The fact is that what most of them refer to as hairball coughing, is not related to hairballs at all. As noted, hairballs are hard, usually columnar masses of hair that can occasionally be vomited up. Remember, cats are constantly ingesting fur as they groom themselves; during surgery we generally find some hair in the stomach, usually in the form of a loose clump. When cats vomit, you frequently find some loose nests of hair, but generally not the solid mass of a true hairball. Hairballs can be regurgitated, vomited, or retched up, but they can't be coughed up. Coughing is generally related to respiratory or heart problems.

Are Hairballs Ever Dangerous?

In very rare instances, an oversize hairball will get caught in the stomach or small intestine. This rapidly becomes a medical emergency. Symptoms include frequent vomiting, sometimes even vomiting water, and the inability to hold anything down. The cat will lose its appetite and become lethargic, and if not treated within forty-eight hours the intestine will lose its motility and become devitalized.

Don't worry, the chance your cat will have a devitalized intestine is very small. Having a devitalized intestine means that intestine may have suffered damage to its nervous system or compromised its blood flow and is deteriorating. While it is rare, this condition does require surgery, as it's the only way of removing the blockage.

Does It Hurt My Cat to Vomit Up a Hairball?

It's actually good for cats to get rid of a hairball by vomiting. If your cat regularly vomits up hairballs, you may consider Furball Preparations—this is not a joke—like Laxaire, Petromalt, and Laxatone, which are all available through a vet or at most pet shops. These are tube-dispensed gels. At The Cat Practice we generally use Laxaire as cats seem to prefer the taste. These remedies will work about half the time. But the best way to eliminate the problem is to thoroughly brush or comb the cat's coat every other day, in addition to a taste of Laxaire. Vitamins and a good diet will help keep your cat's coat nice as well as prevent excess shedding.

Cat Stat

The ability to vomit easily and often is part of a cat's defense mechanism. It helps protect them from being poisoned by a plant. A cat will almost immediately expel by vomiting anything toxic or irritating. Outdoor cats, who basically limit their food to, well, *everything* are rarely poisoned. Most of the patients I see that have eaten a poisonous or otherwise dangerous plant are indoor cats that have eaten an ornamental plant. The only truly serious case of plant poisoning I have treated in nearly thirty years of exclusively feline medicine involved Easter Lilies. For some reason no one seems to be able to explain, cats don't seem to be able to vomit them up, and the consequences can be deadly. No cat household should have any member of the Lily family in the environment. Period. It's lilies or your cat's life.

How Much Vomiting Is Too Much?

If your cat vomits continuously for more than twenty-four hours, go see your vet. A vet can administer antivomiting injections to bypass the irritated stomach and may give your pet Barium, which coats the stomach to break the vomiting cycle. The Barium's passage to the colon will help the vet rule out an obstruction.

What Is a Vacuum Cleaner Cat?

Vacuum cleaner cats, as we refer to them in the office, are prone to rejection vomiting. The solution is an obvious one: Switch to canned food, or simply feed your cat smaller portions more frequently.

MEOW! "Give a cat a fish and you feed her for a day; teach a cat to fish and she will wait for you to feed her."

—HBS

Do Cats Have Food Allergies?

You may assume that cats love fish. In fact, many cats are allergic to fish. Contrary to what many people believe, seafood is not a natural food for cats. Not all cats, but a surprisingly large number of cats will have an obvious reaction to fish. Let me put it this way: Among the more popular canned pet foods are tuna and salmon. And when was the last time you saw any member of the cat family catching a tuna? Seafood is to some degree a convenience food for pet food manufacturers. It is a cheap source of protein and has a strong taste—you often know it when you open the can—which some cats love.

Cat Tip: Many cats prone to vomiting improve markedly as soon as seafood is eliminated from their diet. So if you're one of those cat owners who needs to be careful where you walk at night when you get out of bed, read the ingredients on cat food cans and try a fish-free diet for three weeks to see if it helps.

Cat Stat

There is a theory that outdoor cats eat grasses on purpose, knowing instinctively that this will initiate vomiting that rids them of the hairball. Yet statistics show that when there are other foods available, cats will eat only about 10 percent vegetable matter; when small game isn't readily available, cats will eat as much as 35 percent grasses and other vegetable matter.

When Is a Cough Not a Hairball?

So what is causing your cat to cough and hack as if something is caught in its throat? Okay, just think of what your cat looks like when you think it's hacking up a hairball: His chin is down close to the ground, his neck is extended, and his abdomen and chest are heaving. The sound of the cough can be varied; it can be a snort, a honk or most often, a wheeze. It can be dry, meaning nothing is coughed up, or wet. If it is wet or productive, unlike a hairball, it usually results in the cat coughing up mucus or other fluids.

cat tales: While I was a student at Cornell I worked in the postmortem lab doing autopsies. Because of my interest in cats, I autopsied or "posted" nearly every deceased cat that arrived, which was probably close to nine hundred total. I can't remember finding hair in a single windpipe, which would be the only reasonable explanation for hairball hacking.

What Do I Do If My Cat's Cough Persists?

A persistent cough should never be ignored or simply chalked up to a hairball. It's rarely a hairball. Persistent coughing in cats will require a trip to your vet. To determine the source of a cough, chest X-rays are going to be necessary.

The causes, in order of frequency are:

1. asthma-bronchitis complex
2. asthma
3. bronchitis
4. pneumonias bacterial, fungal or viral trachectis
5. heart disease
6. space occupying respiratory lesions: abscesses, granulomas, benign or malignant tumors

What Does Blood in the Litter Box Mean?

This is a question I hear a lot, usually from panicked clients. As all cats know, their owners are creatures of habit and anything they find out of the ordinary will set them off running around the house in a nervous frenzy. But as it turns out, blood in a cat's stool is not all that unusual. At least 90 percent of the time it's due to impaction and/or inflammation of the two anal sacs, which sit at 3 o'clock and 9 o'clock in relation to the anus.

Every time feces pass through the cat's anus, these anal glands or anal sacs leave a few drops of oily, incredibly heinous musk. Occasionally, these glands will not discharge and the musk will back up.

Cat Stat

These blueberry-size glands are extremely important to cats—they serve as sensory "fingerprints," a method of identification, for other cats. These glands secrete a musk that gives each cat's bowel movement a distinct odor. This enables other cats to identify if interlopers are infringing on their territory. This may well be at least a partial explanation of why cats go to the trouble of burying their feces.

Eventually it will begin to harden, making it even more difficult for it to be expelled through very narrow ducts. The gland may actually rupture and cause subcutaneous infection or abscesses that will erode through the skin. These abscesses often need to be surgically cleaned out.

Seriously, Am I Really Supposed to Squeeze My Cat's Butt?

Even a modest swelling of these glands can cause a local inflammation in the end of the colon, which often results in the fresh blood and/or mucus that is

visible on the stool. This symptom is usually pretty easily cured by manually squeezing the gland, which I do about a dozen times a day—on a good day. Well, an average day. Squeezing a cat's rear is not the definition of a good day. This is a somewhat arcane skill that your vet can show you how to do—if you have a strong stomach. Rubber gloves are an absolute necessity unless you plan on spending the next week washing your hands.

MEOW! "If a dog jumps in your lap, it is because he is fond of you; but if a cat does the same thing, it is because your lap is warmer."

—Alfred North Whitehead

What Does It Mean When My Cat Scoots on His Behind?

The symptoms most often associated with anal gland disturbances are varied. One of the most common symptoms is called scooting. You know this one because it looks a little funny: It's when a cat drags its butt across the floor. What it's trying to do is get the gland to empty. Other signs may include feces being half-in and half-out of the litter box or the cat walking out of the box with stool protruding from its rectum; constipation; and yes, unfortunately, urinary indiscretions.

Do Cats Get Hemorrhoids?

If you notice blood in your cat's stool take him to your vet for the relief both of you need. The vet will empty those sacs. He will also examine the rectum for hemorrhoids, but I've only seen a half-dozen cats with 'rhoids over the years. Perhaps it's rare because cats generally avoid wasabi, fire-wings, Szechuan chicken, and chili dogs. Maybe they know something we don't.

Do Cats Need Health Insurance?

Health care costs for pets are on the rise: A trip to the emergency room can run as much as $800 or more. That's why pet insurance is a rapidly growing industry in this country. There are several different companies offering a variety of policies. For years I've been reading about medical doctors being deluged with forms and, admittedly, chuckling. But you know what, I'm beginning to understand it—and it isn't that funny. I'm still getting accustomed to filling out forms— although it hasn't reached the point at which they tell me what tests I can conduct and whether surgery is warranted or not.

How Reliable Is Pet Insurance?

Because it is such a new industry, there are a lot of problems with it. It can be beneficial for you under the right circumstances, but at this point it is probably less than meets your wallet. Most policies do not cover pre-existing conditions, which are often chronic problems. If, for example, your cat has had a single urinary problem in its life, the insurer might not cover it for any and all other urinary problems—which are frequent. Personally, I'm ambivalent. There are some advantages. You'll probably never be reimbursed the full amount of your vet bill, but hey, 75 percent of a $5,000 bill might still make it very worthwhile to have the policy. Psychologically you may also find opportunities to bring your pet into the vet at times you might otherwise have decided not to spend the money. I would definitely look into it, and even if you decide it isn't worth it for you right now, I would keep track of the offers because they will change as the industry matures. If you have a young cat, insurance is worth investigating because the rates are less expensive than for older cats and it's likely your young cat has few, if any, preexisting conditions.

How Good Is Pet Insurance Coverage, Really?

The basic truth: Pet insurance rarely covers everything you might assume it would cover. The first question you should ask a pet insurance agent is whether or not the company covers routine physical examinations and vaccinations. To make it worthwhile, these procedures should be covered, because over several years these necessary visits to your vet will add up to a significant

Cat Stat

One way to determine if pet insurance is for you is to talk to pet owners who have used it. You can find these people by hanging out in the pet food aisle of your local supermarket. Just ask them if their pet is insured and then get the details. How do they feel about the company? Have they spent more for the policy than they recovered?

amount of money. Find out if the policy covers dental cleaning. This is another common expense and, because it requires anesthesia, can be as expensive—or even more expensive—as a visit to your own dentist.

You should also find out if there are upper limits in the reimbursement offered for each incident during the life of the policy. A serious sickness or injury can cost thousands of dollars over a relatively brief period of time. Other treatments, like cancer, are both expensive and prolonged. So begin by finding out specifically what costs are covered.

What about Pre-existing Conditions?

Now, some insurers will cover pre-existing conditions, but most don't. When my clients buy this insurance I will be asked to sign off on whether or not certain conditions are present. That puts me in an unpleasant position, but I have to be completely honest as insurers can request all medical records.

Like human insurance, most pet insurance companies will have guidelines as to what a specific illness or procedure should cost. For example, the insurance company may decide that a urinary blockage requiring catheterization, hospitalization, and treatment for four days should be billed at, oh, $600. This figure may be based on national or state averages, but what costs $600 in upstate New York will certainly be more expensive in Manhattan. So the maximum coverage offered by the company may be less or even considerably less than the cost of a procedure.

Do I Have to Have My Cat Altered?

The sad truth is that shelters are forced to put thousands of unwanted felines to sleep each year, so it serves all of us to make sure our cats do not breed and add to this problem. There are so many cats—and kittens—in shelters needing good homes that we all need to provide better birth control for our pets. That means cats should be spayed or neutered as early as possible.

Cat Stat

Believe it or not, cats can become pregnant as young as four-and-a-half months of age, although generally that first pregnancy takes place somewhere between six months and a year. At The Cat Practice, we recommend altering a cat at six months. Shelters, however, will neuter cats as young as four months and, occasionally, even younger to make sure they will never breed in their new homes.

How Can I Tell When My Cat Is Pregnant?

Here's what you should know: A female cat's gestation period is about sixty-two days. Often for the first month a pregnant cat will show little or no change in her behavior or appearance. During the second month, she will grow larger in the abdominal region and her nipples will become progressively more prominent.

Is There a Pregnancy Kit for Cats?

Unfortunately, there is no early pregnancy kit for cats. If you need to confirm that your cat is pregnant or how many kittens she is going to have or when her litter is due, take the cat to the vet. It's usually best to avoid aggressive palpation and X-rays because they can damage the fetuses. Abdominal ultrasound can answer these questions—but it's expensive.

Can I Take a Lamaze Course With My Cat?

That won't be necessary. But you can help your cat prepare for the birth of the litter. About a week before delivery, your cat will finally begin to nest. Usually she'll find an out-of-the-way, well-protected spot. She'll gather soft materials, cloth or paper, and build a small birthing haven for herself. Unfortunately, the father will be nowhere to be seen. By this time she will be fairly rotund and her nipples will be very prominent.

Does a Pregnant Cat Eat for Two . . . or Ten?

The most common litter size is four to five kittens, although cats are capable of giving birth to as many as ten kittens. Like any mother eating for ten, she will want to eat more. A lot more. And with her increased metabolic rate, she is going to need additional nutrition as well. If your cat does not develop diarrhea from dairy products, providing milk regularly will ensure that she has adequate calcium reserves for parturition—that is, giving birth and nursing. If she is lactose intolerant, you might try lactose-free milk.

How Do I Coach Her through Labor and Delivery?

The very best thing you can do to help your cat through this miraculous process is to be a cautious observer. Don't intervene. As much as you want to assist her, don't. Cats have been doing this for eons without your help, and your cat can handle this on her own.

Cats have the ability to control the timing of their delivery, so often she will give birth in the early morning hours when the house is quiet. The first sign you may get that the event had taken place may well be in the morning when the lady shows up for breakfast with a new, slim waistline. Feed her, she's had a rough night, then check her backside to see if there is any vaginal discharge or anything like retained placenta hanging out of her. If there is, just gently clean her.

MEOW! **"A kitten is in the animal world what a rosebud is in the garden."**

—Robert Southey

Does a Mommy Cat Need Help Nursing?

It's okay to take a cautious glance at her nest to see the kittens, but as hard as it is to resist, it's much better not to get too close or handle them at this point. Just watch to make sure that the new mother is nursing her brood. The first several successful nursing's will give the kittens much-needed colostrum, a mixture that provides them with protein as well as the antibodies necessary to protect them from infectious diseases to which their mother has developed an immunity either through natural exposure or vaccinations.

Hopefully, she is also providing an adequate supply of milk. You actually should notice a swelling of the mammary tissue in a quarter-size area around each of her eight nipples. All of her mammary tissue may not be activated, but there should be at least one engorged breast for each kitten. You can gently press the breast and see if a small drop of milk appears. This should reassure you that all is well. Just remember, this discharge on the first day will be thick with colostrums, so it may appear to be more opaque than milky. Don't worry about it, it's normal.

Do Mommy Cats Get Post-Partum Blues?

If your cat is acting normally, eating well, and nursing her kittens, things are probably fine. But if she has delivered her litter and still seems to be in labor, meaning she stays in the nest, doesn't eat well, and seems to be getting weaker—don't panic! Give her several more hours as sometimes there will be a long pause in the birthing process. But if the situation persists for more than six to eight hours it may be necessary to bundle up Mom and her newborns—preferably in their nest—and seek emergency help.

How Warm Must the Newborn Kitties Be?

Newborn kittens need warmth. This is critical. Generally, if you're warm enough, then probably the temperature in the nest is adequate. Remember, the nest has been built for warmth in a draft-free spot, and the mother is radiating her natural 102-degree temperature to keep her kids toasty.

When Will a New Mommy Cat Let You Touch Her Kittens?

Cat Stat

If the new mother decides that her nest is no longer safe for her children, she will move them to a new locale. If this happens you probably will see her gently carrying them one-by-one. That probably is a sign you're spending too much time with the kittens, so if this happens — no matter how well meaning you are — back off a bit.

The new mother will let you know when it is permissible to inspect the neonates more closely. They will grow quickly, but their eyes will stay closed for as long as ten to fourteen days. When they first open, the kitten's eyes will be blue, but shortly after the first month its eyes will change slowly to their permanent color. When you have her permission, handle these kittens very carefully. Wash your hands before touching them and do not take them away from their nest.

How Much Can a Nursing Cat Eat?

More than you'd imagine. The best thing you can do for your mommy cat is feed her. A lot. Once she starts nursing she is expending a tremendous amount of calories, so the best thing you can do is provide her with food and milk. It's very easy for a nursing mother to become calcium deficient.

When Do Kittens Start Eating Solid Food?

At around six weeks of age, the kittens will become interested in solid food and start exploring. This is the time for you to start looking for good permanent homes, but it's best if they remain with their mother and the litter until they're four months old as valuable socialization occurs between eight and sixteen weeks.

MEOW! **"A kitten is chiefly remarkable for rushing about like mad at nothing whatever, and generally stopping before it gets there."**

—Agnes Repplier

Chapter 5:

Emergency!

MEOW! "Take a cat, nourish it well with milk and tender meat, make it a couch of silk . . ."
—Geoffrey Chaucer

There are emergencies and then there are cat emergencies. Cats may call a state of emergency for reasons we humans may not understand:

Top Ten Cat Emergencies
1. You're out of cream.
2. You're out of Fancy Feast.
3. You're out of catnip.
4. It's been twenty minutes since you've been stroked.
5. It's been twenty minutes since your litter box was cleaned.
6. It's been twenty minutes since you've had fresh food.
7. There's a dog in the house.
8. There's still a dog in the house.

9. Your human won't sit still long enough for you to curl up in its lap.
10. Your human won't lie still enough for you to sleep on its head.

Cat Stat

Most experts believe the closest wild relative to our domestic cats is the Sand Cat from the deserts of Libya and Tunisia. And they are particularly well suited to be cool cats. Many people wonder why members of the cat family vary in so many ways. The answer is they are usually designed for their environment. For example, cats like the Maine Coon and the Norwegian Forest Cat have long, thick fur with a heavy undercoat to provide them with sufficient insulation against long, cold winters. Their coats are often dark, as dark absorbs heat. Cats that have adapted to tropical regions have shorter, finer hair and often have a scant or absent undercoat. They are usually fair or pale in color—think about the lions and leopards from the veldt. Black leopards are the genetic exception to the rule. Sand Cats are well adapted for hot and dry climates: Their short hair, almost nonexistent undercoat, and lighter colors keep them cool.

What Is the First Sign of Illness in a Cat?

The first symptom of illness in a cat is behavior. If your cat suddenly seems lethargic, particularly when offered food, and its ears are warm there is a pretty good chance he is running a high fever. Just as we get slow and achy when we have a fever, so do cats:

Their myalgia—muscle aches—and lassitude are very much the same as ours.

cat tales: The difference between humans and cats was made clear to me when I ran my own urine sample at The Cat Practice. I had been concerned about the fact I seemed to be craving more water than ever before and wondered if it might be a sign of diabetes. I found no sugar in my urine, but the concentration—the specific gravity of my urine—was very dilute. If I were a cat, I would have been in serious trouble, suffering from incipient kidney dysfunction. I wasn't sure what that meant, but I didn't think it was good. I immediately called my doctor with the news that I had very diluted urine.

She laughed. I told her the reading and she explained it was within the very normal range for people. "Try to stick with your own species," she advised me. "And diagnose those patients you were trained to treat."

How Hot Is Too Hot?

Physically, cats are hot. Their normal body temperature runs between 100.5 and 102.5 degrees Fahrenheit. You can get a pretty good idea of whether or not your furry friend is running a fever by observing his behavior and feeling his ears. If a cat is calm his ears are usually cool; if the cat is excited, his ears can feel warm. A calm cat with warm to hot ears may be running a fever.

Is a Cold Nose a Good Thing?

Everyone knows that the best way to determine how your cat is feeling is to touch its nose—cold nose, warm nose, dry nose, wet nose. And everyone who knows that is absolutely wrong. That's about as helpful as determining how you feel by touching your own nose. The only accurate way to determine a cat's temperature is with a rectal digital thermometer.

Cat Tip: I never recommend the traditional glass thermometers for two reasons: First, the bulb is usually larger than the new digital thermometers, which makes insertion more difficult for both the inserter and the insertee. Second, and unfortunately this is a lesson I have learned from experience, if your cat suddenly and unexpectedly backs up and sits down, the thermometer can break off in the cat's rectum— and it can be difficult to retrieve with the possibility of very dangerous mercury absorption through the colon.

Trust me, don't use a glass thermometer. Rectal thermometers cost between $7 and $9 and can be purchased at most drug stores. The proper way to take your cat's temperature is explained in "How Do I Take a Cat's Temperature?" on the next page.

When we broke a glass thermometer at The Cat Practice, we immediately had to anesthetize the cat and take her into surgery. We retrieved the thermometer and copiously flushed the colon with warm saline. Fortunately, she wasn't cut and suffered nothing more than embarrassment—but I immediately purchased a large supply of inexpensive plastic digital thermometers.

How Do I Take a Cat's Temperature?

If your cat acts lethargic and/or his ears are warm or hot, then you should take your cat's temperature. You'll need a rectal thermometer. Flexible plastic battery-driven thermometers aren't very expensive and can be found in any drug store. Taking a cat's temperature is a two-person job: One person must secure and comfort the cat in front while one person is in the back. Lubricate the end of the thermometer with KY jelly, Vaseline, or even olive oil and gently insert it about an inch into the rectum. If you encounter resistance try to vary the angle and gently proceed. You should have a steady temperature within a minute or less.

Cat Stat

A cat's normal temperature runs between 100.5 and 102.5 degrees Fahrenheit. A mild temperature increase to 103.5 degrees Fahrenheit is nothing to worry about. A temperature between 103.5 and 104.5 degrees Fahrenheit is a cause for concern, but not yet an emergency unless accompanied by dehydration. Temperatures between 104.6 to 107 degrees Fahrenheit should be dealt with as an emergency, as this can make your charge both dehydrated and miserable. Cats with very high fevers, 106 degrees Fahrenheit and above, often move with reluctance and walk like little old men because of significant muscle aching.

MEOW! "It has been the providence of Nature to give the cat nine lives instead of one."

—Bidpai

Can the Heimlich Maneuver
Save a Choking Cat?

In a recent cartoon, a cat swallowed an entire fish and started choking. A waiter used the Heimlich maneuver on him—and the fish shot across the restaurant straight onto the plate of a woman, who immediately began eating it. Cartoons aside, there are emergency actions you can take to help a cat in distress—but the Heimlich maneuver isn't one of them. In the Heimlich maneuver, you stand behind a choking victim and press in hard under the diaphragm with your fists to force out whatever may be caught in the victim's windpipe. I suppose it could work with cats—the diaphragm is toward the end of its rib cage—but I just don't foresee this being necessary. In more than thirty years I've never seen or even heard of a cat choking on food.

Should I Give My Cat Mouth-to-Mouth?

As disturbed as you may be to hear it, mouth-to-mouth resuscitation can be very effective. Someday it may help you save your cat's life. I've used it several times at The Cat Practice, often coupled with closed-chest cardiac massage. It's not something I recommend unless this is your own cat and it's clearly in distress, because you are bringing a scared animal—along with its sharp claws and teeth—within striking distance of your face and eyes. And a panicked animal will do things that it never would normally do. But if it becomes necessary, grasp the cat's chest with your thumb about even with the fourth rib—a bit forward of the midchest area—and your fingers on the opposite chest wall and rhythmically squeeze the heart every two seconds. In between squeezes, cover the cat's nose and mouth with your lips and blow gently. You should be able to feel the lungs inflating with your hand. It's very important not to blow too hard—just enough to feel movement in the rib cage.

What, Precisely, Constitutes a Life-Threatening Emergency?

With your cat came certain responsibilities, primary among them to provide health care for your feline family member. Normal pet care can be expensive—and emergency care can be very expensive. The reality is that it can be tremendously confusing and stressful trying to decide whether you need to rush your cat to an emergency hospital in the middle of the night or if it's safe to wait until the morning. When you're in doubt, ask. Call the emergency service and describe the symptoms. They are the experts. They'll give you the best possible advice at that moment.

How Do I Know When to Go to the ER, and When to Wait for the Vet?

Most pet owners have a regular vet, but unfortunately very few of those vets are available twenty-four hours a day, seven days a week. Larger veterinary hospitals may well be open for emergencies around the clock, but at smaller clinics like The Cat Practice that's just impossible. Emergency medical care is like the last gas station before the desert—you're going to pay a lot more for services. So before you decide whether it's worth spending the money,

cat tales: A good friend of mine, Gary Zeller, loaned my family his rustic Catskills cabin for the weekend. I wandered into the bathroom and was surprised to find two mice floating in the toilet bowl. The first mouse was clearly dead, its body already in rigor mortis. But the other mouse was not yet rigid: Although he wasn't breathing, his body was still warm. Instinctively I put its tiny face between my lips and very gently and rhythmically started breathing for it, while gently compressing its rib cage. I couldn't feel a heartbeat, but that would be very easy to miss in such a tiny creature.

As I was standing there doing my very best, I glanced at the open doorway. My wife Ginger and daughters were standing there, obviously wondering what I was doing with a mouse in my mouth.

"Just what do you think you're doing?" Ginger asked.

There really aren't a lot of good answers to that question. I said nothing, although if I had been clever I would have told her that I was giving mouth-to-mouse resuscitation.

The mouse began to breathe. It moved, trying to free itself from my grasp. Fortunately, I got it out of my mouth before it could bite me. My daughters were thrilled. "Dad saved Mr. Mouse!" Ginger was not as impressed.

Note: Do not try this at home. Animals and birds do carry disease and they do bite. I saved that mouse long before dangerous infections like the Hanta Virus were fully understood. Truthfully, given the same scenario today, I don't know how I would react.

consider what has happened to your cat and the situation in which you find yourself.

Should Constipated Cats Go to the ER?

This is rarely a problem that can't wait until the next day. There are a few signs to look for: A constipated cat probably won't have much of an appetite. It will also spend a good deal of time straining in or out of the litter box. This straining may result in vomiting. Don't worry, there is plenty of time to watch and wait.

I've seen cats survive days without using their litter box without it being a serious problem. In fact, I've had clients tell me that their cats haven't used the litter box in a week, yet they show no signs that anything is wrong. My response is that they should wait—and for God's sakes check all the potted plants! I also suggest they ask everyone else in the house if they've scooped the box. As the constipation progresses, the cat eventually will start acting a little off. So if he seems lethargic, isn't eating very well, and hasn't used the box, then he should be examined by your vet. But it isn't an emergency and usually it is something that can be treated relatively easily the next morning.

What If My Cat Is in an Accident?

If your cat has been hit by a car or has fallen out of a window or suffered any similar obvious trauma, it needs to be thoroughly checked out as quickly as possible. You may be thinking, *Duh!* The problem is this: After some accidents cats actually can appear to be healthy.

cat tales: My first job out of vet school was at a suburban New York small animal hospital. It was a five-vet practice and when I accepted the job I knew I would be on emergency call every fifth day. I knew that. Unfortunately, just before I arrived the vet-owner fired two vets and then took off for the summer to fish. Like the bad movie cliché, I was going in a rookie, but I was going to come out of it absolutely exhausted. It meant that I was on call every other night. It wasn't unusual for me to work from 9 a.m. to 6 p.m. and then be called back to the hospital at various times throughout the night, right into the morning. After several weeks of this, I was dizzy with fatigue and it was only through the grace of the Almighty that I did not make some catastrophic mistakes. That's when I realized that emergency services are a great and important service—not only to pet owners but also to vets in private practice. I have learned to depend on these vets, who generally provide quality medical care when it's most needed. An emergency service is a fully-staffed 24/7 animal care facility that exists in most larger towns or cities. Most will stabilize your animal and when it is appropriate refer back to the pets' regular vet.

They may walk normally, they may not have any open cuts, and they may act as if everything is fine. However, there are some serious injuries that are not immediately symptomatic. Frequently the impact from a car bumper or hitting a sidewalk on a cat will cause internal injuries, for example a ruptured spleen, internal bleeding, or a burst urinary bladder—and a cat's amazing stoicism may make it appear as if nothing is wrong, or at worst they've suffered minor injuries. These aren't minor injuries; they're life threatening, and a thorough physical examination—including X-rays—may be necessary to uncover these slow killers.

What If My Cat Is Having Trouble Breathing?

When a client calls and reports that his or her animal is having breathing problems, my response is always, "Bring it right in. Now." I've learned that a cat's breathing pattern is usually abnormal long before the client has noticed it. Thus, by the time many cats make it into the office, they are in severe respiratory distress.

My physical exams always start with a careful look at the cat's respiratory rate and effort. Most cats I examine are nervous so I expect their respiratory rate to be fast—forty to sixty breaths per minute—but there is little chest or abdominal movement. Their breathing is shallow, effortless, and rapid. Labored breathing is different. The rate may be accelerated, but there will also be significant movement of the rib cage and abdominal lift as the cat uses its abdominal muscles to help force air in or out of the chest. These pumping respirations are obvious signs that there is a serious problem with the lungs or the heart. Cats will also flare their nostrils when they struggle to breathe. If it has progressed to open-mouth breathing you should asssume the situation is critical. Get help for your animal immediately.

Can I Count My Cat's Breaths?

Count your cat's breaths per minute. One breath equals an inspiration and expiration. Cats normally breathe sixteen to twenty-five times per minute while asleep, resting cats may breath twenty to thirty times per minute, and fully awake and alert cats can take as many as thirty to fifty breaths per minute.

Cat Tip: To evaluate your cat's breathing, the best thing to do is catch your cat napping. Look at his abdomen just behind the ribcage. You should be able to see the movement from a distance so you don't wake him, and then start counting: Here's a simple test—if the breathing seems abnormal to you, it probably is. Call the vet on emergency service.

What Causes a Cat to Have Trouble Breathing?

It's very difficult for a vet to determine what's wrong with a cat by looking at it. Listening to its lungs with a stethoscope may confirm that a problem exists but won't tell what it is. There are many different problems that can cause rapid breathing and increased respiratory effort. These include asthma, bronchitis, asthma-bronchitis complex, heart problems, fever, anemia, pneumonia, lung or chest masses, ruptured diaphragms.

Breathing problems are serious and must be treated immediately. This is definitely a time to take your cat to the emergency room. Most of them can be cured if treated promptly and aggressively. But if they are not treated, it can be fatal. Even the symptoms of more serious problems can be alleviated to ease the burden on the animal before beginning long-term treatment.

Is Asthma Easy to Spot in a Cat?

I can often diagnose the problem by how much difficulty the cat is having moving air in and out of its lungs—that is, inspiratory dyspnea versus expiratory dyspnea. Cats who have trouble pumping the air *out* of their lungs are often suffering from asthma and/or bronchitis. Fortunately, this is often a treatable problem. Cats do respond well and quickly to medication.

> **Cat Stat**
>
> The average cat has a bowel movement daily or every other day. That said, it isn't *that* unusual for cats to have less frequent bowel movements. There are a lot of reasons for this, both environmental and psychological. Cats sometimes delay defecation when they are in a stressful situation. Also, if they don't feel well they eat less, which results in a marked decrease in their need to defecate.

What About Heart Trouble?

When a cat struggles to move air *into* the lungs, he may be experiencing heart problems. The cat's lungs may be filled with fluid because his heart is failing as a pump. X-rays are going to be necessary. Without X-rays it is unlikely that a vet will be able to make a proper diagnosis. Even then, additional testing may be necessary, including blood tests and an ultrasound exam.

What Do I Do When My Cat Is Bleeding?

Serious bleeding is clearly an emergency. Arterial or diffuse bleeding is pretty obvious and requires immediate attention. Treat it the same as you would for a child—with claws. Apply local pressure or tourniquets and rush the cat to the nearest open facility. However, the good news is that most bleeding from lacerations can easily be controlled. If an animals' clotting system is healthy, most bleeding will stop after a short time.

Note that most of the bleeding problems you'll encounter in cats are minor. Cats get scratched or bitten by other cats, or you may clip your cat's nails too close. Generally, applying pressure to the wound will quickly stop minor bleeding. For persistent bleeding, you can salt an ice cube and apply it to the wound. A lot of cats aren't happy with this kind of attention—they like to take care of themselves—but soft words and petting will help.

Can a Cat Get a Bloody Nose?

Cats do get bloody noses. The most common cause is an extreme failure of their four-paw braking system as they race around the house and confront obstacles. Walls, for example. This type of bleeding is almost always self-limiting and doesn't require a trip to the emergency room. I see a lot of cats who have abnormalities of their nasal plane, often the result of a past scrape or accident. Believe it or not, violent sneezing can also cause a slight nosebleed, and nasal or sinus infections may result in the production of bloody mucus. These aren't emergencies and don't require immediate treatment.

Cat Tip: A good rule of thumb: To the nervous cat fancier, the volume of blood loss always seems to be about three or four times greater than it actually is. A teaspoon of hemorrhage can be terrifying when it's coming out of your cat. But it may not be that serious. In a bleeding emergency apply pressure to the open wound, put salt on an ice cube and hold it on the wound for several minutes. This super cooling will often effectively arrest the bleeding.

What Does Blood in a Cat's Vomit Mean?

This isn't uncommon. Violent or repeated vomiting can cause the capillaries in the stomach or esophagus to rupture. Vomit with a pinkish, bloody tinge may be scary, but it's not an emergency. Obviously, large amounts of blood in vomit is an emergency, but that's very unusual.

Do Cats Cry Tears of Blood?

I've rarely seen bloody discharge flow from the eyes unless there is obvious, severe damage to the eye. However, cats' tears often have a reddish tinge that can stain the face—and people often confuse this with a bloody discharge from the eyes.

What Does Blood in My Cat's Urine Indicate?

Whenever a cat develops a urinary tract infection or develops urinary stones or crystals, there is frequently blood present in urine. This too can wait until the next morning.

What Does Blood in My Cat's Poop Indicate?

Anal gland problems often lead to transient inflammation of the colon near the anus and will result in bloody and/or mucus-laden stools. Once again this is not an emergency. Cats do get hemorrhoids, which can produce blood in the feces. Blood from further up in the intestinal tract usually create stools packed with digested blood, which looks a lot like used coffee grounds. If this persists, your cat will require a thorough examination, but if the animal shows no other symptoms it's not an emergency.

What Can Cause Convulsions in Cats?

True seizures in cats need to be thoroughly investigated to eliminate all nonbrain causes. In addition to low blood sugar, possible causes include heart disease, liver disease, anemia, aberrant parasites in the brain, electrolyte deregulation, and others. And you thought cats were easy to diagnose. Believe me, it would help if they could just tell me what hurts. But if all the other causes can be ruled out, then the probability is that the cat is suffering from epilepsy, a disorder of the nerves in the brain.

Will Seizures Kill My Cat?

Convulsions and seizures are not that uncommon in cats. They can be caused by a bewildering collection of diseases. While they're very scary to watch, the good news is that most of the time they're not life threatening. Even so, it's best not to wait to start the whole diagnostic process. The first thing I look for when presented with a cat exhibiting these symptoms is low blood sugar, which is common in diabetic cats who have received too much insulin. It's easy to test for and easy to treat with the intravenous administration of a dextrose solution.

Most seizures last thirty to ninety seconds—or as far as the owner is concerned about a lifetime. I often have people tell me the seizure lasted four or five minutes, which is highly doubtful. More likely, these people confused the seizure with feline fainting.

Do Cats Faint?

Cats do faint. When a cat vomits violently, all its blood becomes pooled in the intestine and the brain is temporarily deprived of blood, so dizziness and fainting can result. I don't want to get personal here, but think back to that New Year's Eve party or that night in college when after having way too much to drink it suddenly seemed like a great idea to put underwear on a Civil War statue or wrap a police car in toilet paper—and just as the plan was hatched you became nauseous and keeled over. Basically you were out like a baby for a brief period of time. It's a similar process; both situations result gastro-intestinal irritation, vomiting and blood pooling in the GI system, leaving the brain short of oxygenated blood.

Why Would a Cat Need a CAT scan?

Convulsive cats might well require an MRI or CAT scan—that's right, your cat can get a CAT scan, although dogs can get CAT scans too—and a sampling of the cerebrospinal fluid can rule out encephalitis, meningitis, or masses in the brain such as a tumors or an abscess. These tests are expensive even during normal business hours and, believe it or not, we often see cats that have negative findings on all these tests. Some of these animals have as many as three seizures and never show any other symptoms despite not being on any anti-seizure medication. Cats with seizures of increasing frequency or duration may need to be placed on Phenobarbital tablets to control their seizures. So, an emergency? If this is the first seizure it does constitute an emergency as it might represent low blood sugar, heart problems, high fever, or severe anemia, which all need to be addressed immediately. If your cat has previously been diagnosed with one of these problems it remains an emergency. However, if your cat has been diagnosed as an epileptic, and suffers a *brief* seizure, it is probably not life threatening.

Can Diarrhea Prove Life Threatening?

Diarrhea is messy but never an emergency unless it persists for forty-eight hours, in which case it can lead to dehydration—and dehydration can be an emergency. What I do when confronted by this problem is put the cat on a combination of turkey baby food mixed 50-50 with well-cooked brown rice. Both of these ingredients are mildly constipative and may firm up the stool quite nicely.

Is Dehydration a Sign of Serious Illness?

You should suspect dehydration if your cat is not eating, is feverish or vomiting, and/or has diarrhea. A cat can become dehydrated in as little as twenty-four hours. Dehydration *is* definitely an emergency and can quickly be remedied with subcutaneous (under the skin) fluids or I.V. (intravenous fluids) injection at your local emergency practice. Remember, most victims of dysentery used to die before it was discovered that simply controlling dehydration would save the life of most victims.

Cat Tip: You can easily check for dehydration at home. Pinch the skin on your own upper forearm and pull it up, then let it go. It should elastically snap down with a ripple. This indicates normal skin tension and rules out dehydration. If the skin is slow to recoil, dehydration may be present. Now do the same thing with your cat. The best place to try this elasticity test is on the cat's back near its shoulder blades—behind the neck on the uppermost part of the cat's body. Then try to rub your finger inside your cat's cheek to see if it's dry. That's a pretty good test— and even better if you can perform it without getting bitten. If the skin does not seem to be elastic and its mouth is dry, there is a reasonable chance your cat is dehydrated and should be seen by a vet quickly

Do Cats Get Ear Infections?

Ear infections do not require emergency treatment unless your cat also demonstrates imbalance or circling, which can mean the problem is affecting the middle and inner ear structures. Swelling of the ear pinnae (the erect cartilaginous pointed ear) is common and usually is the result of an ear infection or ear mites, which will cause the cat to dig at his ears with his back claws. This may be the cause of bleeding inside the ear flap and produce a bloated, rounded pinna. This is unsightly, but, good news, it's not an emergency.

Why Do Cats Get Fevers?

A fever is an important weapon in a cat's—and a human being's— defense system. A lot of bacteria can't survive extreme temperatures, so the body heats up in an attempt to destroy the invaders. A fever can be a very cool thing—but its presence indicates something is wrong. When a normally spirited cat suddenly becomes a couch potato and either doesn't move or moves lethargically or hesitantly as if it were walking on eggs, we can suspect a fever.

Cat Tip: You actually should start by feeling your cat's ears. The best way to check the ears is by pressing your lips against them, as lips have the best temperature sense. Normal feline ears always feel warm—remember, a cat's body temperature is about 3 degrees above ours. If the ears feel too warm, or even hot, the cat might indeed have a fever. Of course, they could also be hot because they're in your mouth, making your cat very nervous and therefore pushing a lot of blood to the periphery of his body— the ears.

When Is My Cat Frolicking— or Falling Over in a Faint?

Unless this is a direct result of vomiting, this is definitely a cause for worry. It can be the result of a diabetic cat getting too much insulin, severe anemia, low blood pressure, stroke, an altered electrolyte (potassium) or a liver problem. This is an emergency and should be treated as such.

They Say Cats Always Land on Their Feet — So Do They Break Their Bones?

Sticks and stones . . . and trees and open windows and so many other accidents . . . may result in broken or cracked bones, even for the most agile cat. If the bone has pierced the skin, then it is an emergency, but this happens very rarely. Believe it or not, most fractures, whether simple or complex, don't require immediate attention. A limping cat may or may not have fractured a leg bone, but generally we prefer to wait a day or two for the swelling to subside before casting or splinting. If it is a really bad break, you may have to discuss surgery options.

Why Is My Cat Having Trouble Walking?

If your cat suddenly loses the use of both back legs, get it to the emergency room as quickly as possible. *This is a real emergency.* There are two common causes of this, and one of them is grave. Cats with undetected heart disease can form clots in the expanded heart chambers, then expel these clots down the aorta. The aorta divides into two main arteries that nourish the back legs. These legs become starved for oxygenated blood and rapidly become cool and then cramp. This is very painful for the cat.

How do you know if this is coronary event? Your cat's rear footpad may appear darker in color than the front pads and will be cool compared to the normal temperature of the front pads. This will be one of the first things the vet will look for. He or she will then palpate, or feel for, the absence of a femoral pulse—the regular beating of the artery on the inside of the thigh. The prognosis for the condition is serious: When it's severe there isn't much that can be done to treat it.

If your pet has lost the use of his hind legs yet has normal circulation, this probably will be a low-back spinal problem from a slipped—malpositioned—disc or spinal fracture. This is certainly serious and requires immediate attention, but at least the prognosis is better. It's guarded, but not grave and with proper diagnostics and treatment the cat can regain complete use of its limbs.

Why Is My Cat Yellow?

If your cat's skin has a yellow tinge—and it may actually appear to be orange, this is an emergency. A cat's skin should light pink, not at all yellow. You usually can see on the bare skin of the ears or in the bald area between the cat's ear and eye. It can also be seen in the roof of the mouth and probably, the most obvious, in the whites of the eyes. This is definitely an emergency because by the time the untrained observer (that's you) notices jaundice, it's usually well advanced.

Jaundice results from dysfunction in the liver–gall bladder–intestinal axis. It can be caused by several different problems of varying severity, including gallstones or obstruction, liver disease, or duodenal tumors. More rarely it can represent wide-scale destruction of red blood cells—destructive anemia—and needs to be addressed quickly with blood tests. It is very important that your jaundiced cat receive immediate treatment while the tests progress. In vet school we used to say, "A yellow cat is a dead cat." Fortunately, this is no longer true.

Is My Cat Really Crazy?

There is such a thing as Crazy Cat! In this case, it's defined by stupor, severe behavioral changes, and frenzied activity. As every cat owner desperate for affection—or even just acknowledgment that they exist—knows, cats display a plethora of moods and varied behaviors, but if your cat suddenly begins to act differently than normal you might be dealing with the results of metabolic or brain disease. For example, if your cat is hard to rouse and unresponsive or only somewhat responsive to strong stimuli, there may be a serious problem. If a cat suddenly starts repetitive motions like circling or paddling while lying down this can be the result of brain problems. Cats with severe toxicity from kidney failure will appear to be very unresponsive. This is an emergency and your cat should be seen right away.

Can a Cat Sneeze Itself to Death?

Occasional sneezing is totally normal in cats—although rarely caused by an allergy to . . . cats. Everyone is familiar with the expression, "Curiosity killed the cat," and while probably not true, curiosity can be the cause of sneezing. Cats are scent detectives: They are inquisitive creatures always investigating their environment. This means smelling everything—including the dust kittens under your bed. Prolonged sneezing can be the result of an allergy or the beginning of an upper respiratory disease—that is, a cat cold. Sometimes the sneezing can be paroxysmal—strings of four to ten sneezes in rapid succession. Usually sneezing produces a fine spray and is not an emergency.

MEOW! **"A cat sneezing is a good omen for everyone who hears it."**

—Italian Saying

What's Wrong if My Cats Swells Up?

Thankfully, swelling without any accompanying symptoms is rarely an emergency. This can result from any trauma, ranging from a bee sting on the face to, more seriously, cancer. Swelling may appear suddenly, acutely, or be chronic—slowly developing—in nature. Swelling can usually wait until the next day when your regular vet is available for treatment—but if it persists, it really should be treated rapidly.

- Swelling of the face, especially in the area under the eye, usually is caused by a root abscess of the back upper tooth, with a secondary infection of the sinus cavity under the cat's eyes. This may be painful for the cat, but it's not an emergency that needs to be treated that night.
- Swelling of a limb can be the result of a fracture, joint infection, subcutaneous (under the skin) bleeding, or abscesses and masses. Again, not an emergency.
- Swelling around the eye usually results from an eye infection with conjunctivitis. If the eyeball is intact and looks normal, this can wait.
- Swelling along an incision is not at all unusual after surgery. If, however, your cat has had abdominal surgery—if it's been spayed or had another invasive procedure—and there is significant swelling this could be the result of dehiscence, or an opening of the abdominal incision, and would constitute an emergency.
- Swelling of the abdomen is usually a slowly building scenario and rarely constitutes an emergency, but if your cat has been unobserved for a while and shows significant distention of its abdomen, it should be seen as quickly as possible as this could represent an accumulation of gas or fluid inside the abdomen, and quickly starting diagnostics and treatment could result in a big advantage in the cat's eventual recovery.

- Swelling around the anus can represent severe constipation with perianal, herniation, or anal gland abscess. Usually this is not an emergency.
- Swelling under the skin can be caused by abscesses, subcutaneous bleeding, benign and malignant masses and wounds, but only rarely is it an emergency.

Cat Tip: Collecting a urine sample from a cat can be difficult—most cats don't like to urinate into a little plastic bottle—but even a small amount of it can be very helpful. You might be able to siphon some of it from a hard surface like wood or linoleum flooring or a plastic bag—some cats like to pee on plastic left on the floor—with a syringe, an eyedropper, or a turkey baster for example. This next suggestion can be a little messy, but you might be able to wring a small amount out of a T-shirt or other piece of clothing that your cat has soiled.

When Is Cat Pee Too Much Cat Pee?

Urinary tract infection and inflammation are common in all breeds of cats. The symptoms are frequent urination with straining—sometimes in the litter box and sometimes on your best oriental rug. You may note that the scant urine is blood-tinged or even contains small granules that look like salt. The cat will often lick frequently at its genital area and appear restless and uncomfortable. As the problem worsens, the amount of urine produced becomes progressively smaller in volume and requires seemingly more effort. Unless the cat is producing drops of urine with frequent, increased effort this is not an emergency, especially if your cat is female. This is a problem that easily can be dealt with by your vet during normal hours. When you see your vet, be sure to try to bring a urine sample, as this will help your vet determine what caused the problem, how to cure it, and how to prevent it from reoccurring.

What's Sex Got to Do with It?

Feline urologic syndrome (FUS) can become a medical emergency if the cat's outflow tract becomes blocked by crystals, stones, or blood clots. This type of blockage is rare in female cats because their urethra is much wider than the organ that runs through a cat's small penis. This straining behavior will usually build up over a day or two, which gives you plenty of time to avoid the late-night trip to the emergency hospital—but sometimes you miss this progression because you were distracted or away.

If your male cat is posturing to urinate but not producing any urine, or just scant drops, then you do have an emergency. This is usually accompanied by the typical lack of interest in food; in addition, the cat may appear to be depressed or anxious. Try picking up the cat with your hands beneath its abdomen. If your cat is having urinary tract difficulties it may display some form of discomfort. Here's the danger: When a cat does have an obstruction the back pressure damage to kidney function can start setting in within a day and within forty-eight hours can prove fatal. So if your male cat is unable to urinate, rush him to the hospital. He will need treatment to relieve the obstruction and to help his waning kidney function.

cat tales: A cat sitter was caring for an altered male cat of a client of mine. She was only going into his apartment twice a day to feed the cat, so she didn't notice the symptoms the cat probably was displaying. But one afternoon she called me in a panic because the cat was barely able to stand. I had her bring the cat over and as soon as I saw him it was obvious he was in serious trouble. He was extremely unresponsive: He couldn't stand up, he was 12 percent dehydrated, and his body temperature was 90 degrees Fahrenheit. As I suspected, he was blocked and probably had been for almost forty-eight hours. He was pretty close to death. He was catheterized, which means a hollow sterile tube was passed through the obstruction in his penis and then we aggressively treated his uremic shock. It really was a close call, but he survived. The point is that you should never wait to seek help when a male cat cannot urinate.

Why Does My Cat Sometimes Look Like He's Playing a Violin?

Your cat is pressing its chin against the bib area of its chest. It looks strange. And if it happens frequently or persistently, it may mean that your cat is experiencing chest pain— angina. This is an indication of a heart problem, a vitamin B1 deficiency, low blood potassium, or even fractured neck vertebrae. All of these causes, except the vitamin deficiency, are enough to constitute an emergency. Because you can't determine the cause by yourself, you should get your cat to the vet as quickly as possible.

Is My Cat's Meow Off-Key?

Yes, it might be! Your cat's meow will change under certain circumstances. A hoarseness or altered pitch may indicate tonsillitis, pharyngitis, or other local problems in the throat. These do not constitute a serious problem, however, and can wait until your vet is back in the office.

When Is a Skinny Cat Too Skinny?

Weight loss usually indicates a problem, although it may happen so slowly over time that you don't even notice it. That's why the first thing I do when examining a cat is weigh it, then compare that weight to its prior weight. Weight loss can be an important symptom of something more severe, but it's not an emergency by itself.

MEOW! **"Cats sleep fat and walk thin."**

—Rosalie Moore

Is That Yowling a Cry in Pain?

Humans may yowl in pain, but cats actually become quiet and withdraw into themselves. Animals in distress "go to ground," meaning they find a safe place to hide. Obviously this makes sense in the wild, where sick or injured animals are at higher risk from predators; being quiet when injured or suffering in silence is a protective mechanism. So, when cats do yowl, it's usually not in pain. That said, if the yowling persists, it may indicate problems such as

> ## Cat Stat
>
> Cats do have a particular yodel—a low-pitched *wow, woow, whoow*—known as a locator call. Kittens make this call when separated from their mothers. A loud cry for assistance, it enables the queen to track down her missing kitten. When an adult cat makes this call, most people believe mistakenly that it is an indication of pain. That's almost never true, so don't be concerned. When your cat cries out and then stops when you call it or pet it, you have unwittingly responded to its locator call: Where are you? What are you doing not paying attention to me?

advanced kidney problems with toxic depression of the brain, feline senility syndrome, high blood ammonia levels, certain vitamin deficiencies, sudden blindness or deafness, and other problems. But while it certainly is distressing to hear, it rarely represents an emergency. Still, you should bring your cat to the vet, as persistent yowling can represent a chronic condition.

Do Cats Suffer Spells of Sudden Weakness?

This is a tough problem to deal with. A sudden and unexplained onset of pronounced weakness should be treated as an emergency, but mild transient weakness can probably wait for the next available appointment.

Are Cats Xenophobic?

Admit it: You never suspected your cat was xenophobic. In fact, you didn't even know what it meant. Basically, it's a fear of strangers. A lot of cats are afraid of Xena, the Warrior Princess, as well as other strangers, especially those with swords and breastplates. It's completely normal behavior and the best thing to do about it is keep your cat out of comic books and gladiator movies.

MEOW! **"A meow massages the heart."**

—Stuart McMillan

Chapter 6:

Please Behave and DON'T MAKE ME BeG

MEOW! **"I gave an order to a cat, and the cat gave it to its tail."**

—Chinese Proverb

You may think your cat lives with you—but the cat may not see it that way. Any self-respecting cat—and there is no other kind—considers itself to be master of its domain. And that includes you. If we are to live happily with cats, we need to understand and appreciate what our cats expect of us. That's why it behooves all us humans to acquaint ourselves with the Cat House Rules.

Cat House Rule No. 1: I am the cat—and you are not.
All of the other Cat House Rules expound on this basic
    principle:
Do keep the food bowl full.
Don't forget to freshen it often.
Do fluff my favorite pillow.
Don't sit on my favorite chair.

Do keep the litter box clean.

Don't forget to change it often.

Do reward me for being me.

Don't forget that I'm the cat—and you are not.

MEOW! **"Even if you have just destroyed a Ming Vase, purr. Usually all will be forgiven."**

—Lenny Rubenstein

Why Is My Cat Asleep One Minute—and Flying from the Chandeliers the Next?

There is a wide range of activity levels among cats. I've had cats with the energy level of a pet rock—although admittedly the rock can be more affectionate. On the other hand, I've also had busy, frenetic, hyperactive cats. And every cat lover has observed this feline pattern of sloth interrupted by sudden and unexplainable bursts of energy—seemingly for no reason. I call this "Crazy Cat Hour."

It may look schizophrenic to us humans, but to the cat it's classic predatory behavior. Felines are the most highly evolved predators on the planet—they literally are designed for hunting. Their flexible bodies, speed, agility, and highly developed senses make it possible for them to hunt and capture prey with remarkable efficiency. Hunting requires prolonged periods of nothing, of just lying in wait, waiting, which is followed by a burst of ferocious activity leading to the kill.

Why Do Cats Sleep So Much?

Cats hunt for food, not sport. So when they have enough food, they are much less likely to hunt. In addition, targets of opportunity may be scarce. During these periods, cats sleep and save energy. So when your cat is fast asleep on your bed he isn't being lazy, he's preparing for the next big hunt to feed you and your entire family.

In prey-free environments—for example, an apartment without any mice—cats lack the opportunity to hunt, but these periods of preparation still have to be supplanted by bursts of activity. What they're doing is mimicking their basic reason to exist—the capture of food.

It *is* possible your cat has seen a ghost, but it is much more likely it is simply venting stored energy according to the pressures of evolutionary adaptation.

cat tales: My clients have shared an amazing array of Crazy Cat Hour theories with me over the years. They vary widely, according to the interests and beliefs of the theorist.

Occultists believe Crazy Cat Hour happens when the cat sees a spirit, ghost, or poltergeist in the environment.

Health- and fitness nuts maintain that Crazy Cat Hour is an aerobic necessity—just the animal keeping in shape.

Vegetarians explain to me that this behavior is caused by a diet high in meat and various by-products.

Cat Stat
House cats average seventeen hours of sleep a day, although they would probably prefer that you think of it as "preparation."

How Do Male Cats Know When a Female's In Heat?

Here's the reality: There is no such thing as abstinence training for cats. And no, she hasn't been reading about Paris Hilton in the tabloids. When your female cat goes into heat she begins broadcasting her availability throughout the whole neighborhood via strong, persistent, pheromone release. Believe me, had she been on satellite radio the message could not have been any stronger. Cats are olfactory Einsteins. Male cats have been prepared by evolution to follow this scent trail for blocks. This might well be where the heat-seeking missile got its name.

> **Cat Stat**
> Another key draw for males is the ready female's constant moaning and keening, which is another sign of a cat in heat.

Do Cats Court Each Other?

It is not at all unusual for multiple intact suitors, toms, to arrive at the cat castle at the same time. There may well be some fighting to see which tom wins the paw of the fair princess. Actually, this is a good thing, aiding in establishing good genes for the kittens, as in breeding by the fittest or, in this case, the toughest.

Are Cats Promiscuous?

Here comes the X-rated part of this book: Female cats are promiscuous. They can't seem to say "neow." They are likely to be bred by several different toms over a short period of time. This insemination

Cat Stat

Female cats are spontaneous ovulators, meaning their eggs are released from the ovaries as a result of intromission. So, once all her eggs are released whether or not they are fertilized, the cat's heat soon ends. Once this business ends, in approximately sixty days, if she is pregnant she will build a nest and give birth to sometimes impossibly varied kittens fathered by possibly many different toms.

by different cats may well reach the multiple eggs the female is releasing and result in her being impregnated by multiple fathers. This is also effective in broadening the gene pool.

What Do Cats Really Like to Play With?

Cats, if they are in the mood, will play with anything—including their own tails. And if they're not in the mood, soft music and chocolates will do no good at all. Basically, cats believe anything left on the floor has been left there for their pleasure and will act accordingly. Say good-bye to that sock. So the question is not so much *what* will cats play with, but rather what *should* they play with.

Do Catnip Mice Make the Best Cat Toy?

From the cat's point of view, the essential cat toy is a catnip mouse. Every cat seems to have one, and most of them are safe enough, but not all of them. From the cat lover's point of view, the verdict is mixed. Depending upon the way the given mice toy is made, it can prove dangerous.

Unfortunately, some are made with small pieces of plastic, especially in the head. As every cat owner knows, the survival time of a stuffed catnip toy is only slightly longer than a super-model's attention span. Any cat worth his heritage is going to chew or kick apart that toy and pieces smaller than a dime could get swallowed or aspirated. Those objects will make it successfully about half-way through the intestine and cause an obstruction that can lead to serious intestinal damage. These life-threatening blockages will require surgery.

cat tales: I've taken a bewildering variety of foreign objects out of blocked cats—and too often the lethal object is identified by the client as part of a catnip mouse. Actually, for precisely this reason we used to make catnip toys for our patients using soft felt filled with catnip, no solid pieces, and a short piece of yarn for a tail. Apparently they worked quite well; we didn't receive a single complaint from our cat customers.

What's the Best Game I Can Play with My Cat?

A perfect gift for your cat, and for you after a long day at work, is a laser pointer. Basically, you sit there and point and your cat chases the light around the room. Cats seem to be curious and fascinated by the light. One word of caution: *Do not* point it directly at your cat, as it can do damage if you shine it directly in its eyes. Cats also seem to be entranced by bobbing toys hanging from a string on the end of a wand or even a piece of wood. You can make one yourself with a sock or buy popular toys like "cat dancer." Just make sure there are no easily swallowed hard interior parts.

Can Cats Fetch?

You should not be ashamed of your cat if it likes to play fetch. Trust me, they have not sold out to dogs. But certain breeds, especially Siamese and related breeds, seem to enjoy chasing soft rubber balls and returning them to their person.

Some very poorly designed cat toys have small silver bells inside so they make noise when they bounce. Do not buy these toys. *Let me repeat that: Do not buy these toys.* These bells are the perfect size to block the intestines if swallowed. About the only good thing I can say about these bells is that they do show up very well on X-rays, making the diagnosis relatively simple.

> ## Cat Stat
> **Cats have forward-facing barbs on the back of their tongue, so it's actually easier for him to swallow an object down his gullet then expel it forward. Any small object that lands in the back of the mouth has an easier journey going down rather than out.**

Should I Let My Cat Play With Rubber Bands?

Many cats love to play with rubber bands. Believe it or not, very small rubber bands are safer, if not completely safe. The longer, wider bands are potential obstructers. Just as you might guess, my daughters owe part of their college educations to the operations I've done removing rubber bands blocking the intestine.

MEOW! "When I play with my cat, how do I know that she is not passing time with me rather than I with her?"

—Montaigne

Cat Tip: Some strings that aren't anchored on the back of the tongue will eventually pass through and be defecated out. Once again a reminder: If your cat has a string sticking out of its rectum, do not pull it out. Do not pull it out. You don't know what it's attached to, so don't pull it out. If your cat is acting normally, it's alert, it's eating and isn't vomiting, you can snip off the end and wait. The continuing motility of the intestine will work on the string if it's not attached. Try this, take a length of string in your hands and rub your hands together—the string will eventually form a ball. If this lump becomes large enough, bigger than a grape, it can cause an obstruction.

Is My Cat's Fascination With Yarn and String Potentially Harmful?

Your cat can play with string and twine and yarn but only if it is under constant observation. These things can very easily become "linear foreign bodies." Too often the string can get hung up on the cat's tongue barbs, while the long end tries to make it through its intestines. Obviously, the longer and thicker the linear object, the greater the chance it will cause an obstruction. This happens so often that numerous veterinary hospitals require examining doctors to note in the record of a vomiting cat "No string under tongue." X-rays on these patients can show that the intestines are plicated—pulled into the pattern of a meandering river. The linear foreign body can eventually saw through the bowel at points of con-

tact because of the constant continuing peristaltic movement
of the intestines.

Can My Cat Play with Thread?

Cats will be attracted to
thread. This can be really
dangerous if that thread is
attached to a sewing nee-
dle. The needle can end up
imbedded in the oral cav-
ity or pass into the stomach or intestine where it
becomes a ticking time
bomb. It'll just be a matter
of time before something

cat tales: Some cats are intrigued by twist ties from the ends of packages and Q-tips and will happily play with them. This is another bad idea. Q-tips will definitely get hung up on the back of the tongue and get swallowed. Sometimes the Q-tip will pass through the intestine, but you can't really count on it. I operated on a cat named Fido, yes Fido, and removed thirteen Q-tips from his stomach. He also had a nice collection of twist ties. Interesting, well interesting to me, the wire center of the twist ties had shown up on the X-rays while the Q-tips had not.

gets punctured, which will lead to very dangerous peritonitis.

Should I Catproof My Home?

Responsible new parents lovingly childproof their home before
bringing home the baby. So before bringing home a kitten or adult
cat, you too should catproof your home. Cats simply don't know
what's good for them—or bad for them.

Check your apartment for these potentially dangerous objects and
put them away. If your cat seems to be fascinated by Q-tips, strings,

needles, twist ties, and wires or any easily obtainable objects, you have to hide and protect these attractive nuisances. You probably should get some safe toys for your cat to play with: Big, soft, and malleable playthings. Truthfully though, you probably don't have to gift wrap them.

cat tales: I remember one cat in particular, owned by a very nice couple. That furry feline had an almost demonic attraction to telephone wires. This proved to be a problem for both the cat and the couple's bank account, as I had to operate three different times to remove telephone wire foreign bodies. After the second operation, I jokingly told the couple I was going to close the incision with Velcro—so I could just dig in every few months to get out all the pieces of wire. Finally they covered every inch of phone, stereo, and computer wiring with Plexiglas tubing.

Is My Cat Deliberately Tripping Me Up?

Some cats excel at tripping humans. In fact, while intellectually I know it's not possible, I do think they rather enjoy it. Oh, maybe not the broken arms and feet that their people suffer, but just the thought that a 175-pound human at the very top of the food chain has to perform a spastic dance, followed immediately by a smacking pratfall—just to avoid their ten-pound bodies. This is the little-discussed secret of pet owners: Animals trip people, people fall down, people break bones. We all know someone who has suffered this indignity.

Amazingly, cats are practically never injured in these accidents. Their lightning-fast reflexes almost guarantee that cats suffer near misses, humans go to the hospital. And then the cat goes to his neutral corner and has a good laugh.

MEOW! **"You own a dog but you feed a cat."**

—Jenny de Vries

Why Would My Cat Try to Trip Me?

Seriously, cats do trip people. Cats want attention and they have only limited means of getting it. For example, they often want to remind their person that, hey, time to put on the old feed bag, time to set the table, hear that growling? It's been three hours since I've eaten so don't you think it's time you filled the old feed bowl? Or perhaps, excuse me, but you haven't told me how beautiful I am and petted me for almost four hours. And by the way, when was the last time you and I played fetch?

How Can I Avoid
Stepping on My Cat?

I'm not sure this is possible. I can't count how many times I have treated cats that have been accidentally stepped on—or cats whose owner believes they have been stepped on. I know there has been a problem, because the owner has come limping into the office. On rare occasions I have seen a fractured tail, but almost always I end up kissing Trippy's head, putting him back in the carrier, and urging the human to get that badly swollen ankle X-rayed.

cat tales: Years ago my wife and I decided it was time to go on a well-earned holiday. We made reservations in the Caribbean. My wife's then-16-year-old brother volunteered to stay at our place and take care of our animals. Because I remembered what I laughingly called "my sense of responsibility" at that age, I made a point of calling at the end of our first day there, just to make sure our house was still standing. "Brother Pete," I began. "How's it going? Are the cat's okay?"

Oh, the cry of anguish that I heard in response. "What's with these critters?" he asked. "Every time I take a step, they're under my feet. The gray one almost tripped me down the staircase. The red one tripped me when I got out of bed this morning. What's going on?"

"They probably just want attention," I explained. "Pet them and talk to them."

It was then he called me crazy for the first time. "I'm too busy getting ice packs for my bruises. I'm a battered catsitter."

"Just try to give them some more attention. Give them some of the catnip I left."

That call surprised me, as neither of my cats were known trippers. So at the end of the second day I called again. "Hey Pete, how's it going today?"

He moaned. "This just isn't working. Not only are they tripping me, the red one is biting my ankles."

I had to think about that for a minute. I was a vet, not a psychiatrist. Red nipping anyone was unusual behavior. I wondered what Pete was doing to get him angry. Then I remembered, the only time he'd exhibited biting behavior was when both my wife and I assumed the other one had fed him. "Wait a second. You're feeding them, right?"

There was a long pause. "Feed them? You didn't tell me that."

A new low in catsitting! I tried to remain calm. "Maybe they're trying to tell you something." *Like, maybe, I'm starving to death, you moronic teenager!*

"Ooohhh. So I was supposed to feed them? Where is their food, anyway?"

Trust me, you do not want to join that large group of cat fanciers who wear a cast as their badge of . . . The Legion of At Least My Cat Survived.

Do Cats Mourn?

A cat's response to the loss of a fellow animal companion, and that includes dogs and other household pets as well as other cats, is as diverse as that of human beings. Believe me, with all the cats we've had, I've seen the entire range of reactions, from the completely ebullient acceptance of the survivor, from "Great, now I get to sleep on the bed and not share the litter box with that rude, nonburying fur bucket," to an actual state of depressed bereavement.

Cats, in general, are upset by big changes. They are the essential creatures of habit. They like to be fed at the same time in the same place and for their environment to remain the same, so anything new or different can create stress. However, this is balanced by their innate ability to live for the moment. They will take advantage of any opportunity at any time in any place.

cat tales: I encountered one episode years ago that convinced me some cats do mourn the loss of a companion. I had taken care of a pair of Siamese named Solomon and Sheba since they were kittens. As many Siamese do, they had formed very strong emotional bonds with each other and their person, a woman named Fran. They were inseparable. They slept wrapped in each other's arms and Solomon always let Sheba eat first. They were constantly involved in mutual grooming and occasional romps around the house. For the first eight years of their life, they had been perfectly healthy, but suddenly Sheba became quite sick. We struggled to save her, but within six weeks she had succumbed to a pancreatic tumor.

Fran reported that after Sheba's death Solomon cried continually, was restless, and roamed around the house in an agitated state. He wasn't interested in being comforted by Fran and refused to eat. I suggested she give him two days, after which his hunger would probably defeat his agitation. Two days later she called to tell me there had been no change in his behavior, so I prescribed some appetite-enhancing pills. The pills made absolutely no difference. This was beginning to get serious.

We tried increasingly potent appetite stimulants: Fran was opening six different cans a day—turkey, pate, roast beef, all his favorites—none of which made the slightest difference.

In my fifteen years of veterinary practice, I had never seen a response this powerful. I began wondering—and worrying—if

Solomon was coincidentally sick. We brought him into my hospital and we did an extensive series of blood tests, urine analysis, X-rays and fecal tests, the whole range of tests that would reveal any kind of medical problem. All of the tests were negative. We went further, conducting an electrocardiogram and even abdominal ultrasound. There was nothing medically wrong with Solomon that I could find.

By that point he had lost almost half his weight. We kept him hydrated and continued to offer him the entire smorgasbord of goodies. Finally, we began force-feeding him, which he tolerated with a detached acceptance—but refused to even pick at anything he was offered.

Finally I sat down with Fran. "I've run every test I can think of," I explained, "from aspergillus to zoonotic diseases and I can't find a thing. Maybe I'm wrong, but this seems to me to be a very strong reaction to Sheba's death. Call it whatever you want, separation anxiety, mourning, but it's serious and life threatening."

As far as I knew there was no such thing as grief counseling for a cat, so I made another suggestion: "The only thing I can think of is to get him a female Siamese kitten." Fran broke all records contacting Siamese breeders and within a day had found a young, healthy feline leukemia- and parasite-free sixteen-week-old female and introduced her to Solomon.

We continued force-feeding Solomon. For the next two days he showed absolutely no interest in the kitten, who really tried to play with him. On the third day he began to watch her antics. On the fourth day he actually baited her with his tail, which was followed soon after with some cautious licks of her squirming body. By the fifth day he was watching her eat, and by the end of the day he was licking his own food. Slowly he regained his appetite and eventually began playing with his new protégé.

Obviously Fran and I were overjoyed. And truthfully, I think the kitten helped Fran get over her own grief at the loss of her beloved companion.

Do cats grieve? Until this case I had never believed it possible. Certainly this was very unusual, but Solomon convinced me otherwise.

How Can I Comfort a Grieving Cat?

The most commonly observed behavior in the survivor when a companion cat dies is restlessness, a transient neediness and perhaps some increased grooming to relieve stress. Believe me, they are not dressing for a funeral. I always tell my clients to pay extra attention to the survivor, maybe give it some extra treats and remove from the environment those items specifically related to the departed cat. Usually this response disappears in a few days or short weeks. In multicat households there may be some sparring or even fighting to reestablish the pecking order. But very rapidly cats will begin to focus on the things that matter most to them: What's for dinner and whose lap is available for naps.

Do Cats Really Hate Mice?

In reality, there is no more enmity between cats and mice than there is between a hammer and a nail. Evolution has enabled rodents to develop those abilities necessary to compete successfully for food with larger animals. In this corner are the mice: They're smart (well, comparatively), fast, and have large litters. They operate quite effectively in the dark and have a strong sense of smell, which enables them to locate even a small crumb or piece of crust. And in the far corner is their enemy, the cats, which have evolved to become the almost perfect predator of mice. Cats also have a great sense of smell, they're quick, and see very well in the dark.

Are All Cats Mousers?

In the cats-versus-mice war, there are some cats who are pacifists. Not all cats are interested in all mice. I've had several cats that happily would watch mice walk by without showing much interest.

Cat Tip: Folklore suggests that if you want a good mouser make sure you get your kitten from a successful mousing mother—it also happens to be true. Kittens learn much of their behavior by watching adults, usually their mother since their father never sticks around. Think about all of those documentaries they made you watch in school that showed the mother cheetah or lioness or bobcat leading her cubs on the hunt so they might learn stalking and capture. House-cat mothers often lack the opportunity to hunt wild prey in an apartment or residential home. If there are mice living in the neighborhood, the mother may wound or partly cripple one and bring it back to her home to allow her uncoordinated offspring to practice.

Do Cats Always Eat What They Catch?

Some cats will eat the entire mouse so you may never even be aware that you have mice. Or rather had mice. Unless you happen to see a tail in the litter box. Obviously well-fed house cats just don't have the incentive to hunt, although some will do so given targets of

Cat Stat

Many cats will also make guttural, singing-like sounds when delivering this prize prey to you. This is the same kind of vocalization heard from those cats that will fetch a toy mouse or other object. I think I can say with some certainty that a hungry cat will not share his mouse, but a well-fed, average house cat, which hunts and kills by instinct rather than for survival, may well choose to deliver this prize to your sneakers.

opportunity. There are few things less appealing to any kind of cat than a cocky mouse.

To someone who cares about life, as I do, it may seem cruel when we watch a cat playing with a mouse, crippling it then letting it go, only to recapture it repeatedly. But for the cat this is necessary survival training. Other cats seem to enjoy bringing the badly wounded or dead rodent to their owner as a gift. Or perhaps a warning: Keep supplying the food or you never know what might happen to you.

cat tales: One of my clients, who lives in an old New York City brownstone, often finds dead mice laid carefully in her husband's sneakers in the morning. She knows who put it there! But she wanted to know what it meant. I told her my theory that some cats will favor their owners with gifts of food to show their appreciation for being fed regularly. Or to prove their ability as hunters. Or maybe they just put it there for safekeeping.

MEOW! "Prowling his own quiet backyard or asleep by the fire, he is still only a whisker away from the wilds."

—Jean Burden

Chapter 7:

Diet

MEOW! **"Cats know how to obtain food without labor, shelter without confinement, and love without penalties."**

— W. L. George

For most cats as well as humans, diet is a four-letter word. Cats will not willingly deprive themselves of food at any time: Why would they? They are bred to hunt, eat, and sleep. Just because your cat lives with you rather than in the wild doesn't mean its priorities have changed. Food is still foremost in its mind—and if in the search for supper your cat has only to hunt you down—rather than a mouse—all the better.

You Know Your Cat Is Hungry If She:
    a)   Waits patiently by her food bowl.
    b)   Meows, meows, meows.
    c)   Rubs against your legs.

You Know You Cat Is *Really* Hungry If She:
    a)   Taps your face with a paw.
    b)   Scratches your face with a claw.

c) Gives up and goes next door to that nicer human.

d) Uses your cell phone to order Chinese.

e) Beats its paws or head against the refrigerator door.

f) You catch it putting salt on the couch.

MEOW! "A cat isn't fussy—just so long as you remember he likes his milk in the shallow, rose-patterned saucer and his fish on the blue plate. From which he will take it, and eat it off the floor."

—Arthur Bridges

Can Cats Eat Anything?

Some cats have no interest at all in "people food." They may be addicted to canned or dry food, probably due to habits formed early in their lives. But more often I meet "The Hoovers," as we call them, cats that will eat anything, and it can be a constant battle of wills keeping them off the counter or the stove or the dining room table.

Can I Train My Cat to Stay Off the Counters?

There is a slight window early in the cat's life when you can stop this behavior by not feeding the cat from the table or counter, or even punishing him or her when they attempt to eat off the table, but after that window has closed you'll be in a long-term battle with your animal. On your side you'll have logic, intelligence, and information. The enemy will have a high cuteness factor and a look of desperation. Forget it, this is a battle you've got no chance of winning.

Look, we all want to satisfy the desires of our cats. That's our job, at least as far as they are concerned. And admittedly, even among those of us who know much better, there is an often over-whelming desire to give your bundle of happiness a treat occa-sionally or every hour, whichever comes first, to keep that tail straight up and reward it for *purrrfect* behavior, cute little licks, and head butts. Okay, do it—but put the treat in the cat dish ON THE FLOOR. Can I make that clear, put food in the cat's dish ON THE FLOOR.

What "People Food" Can I Feed My Cat?

What human treats are good for your cat? Any cooked poultry part is fine—except for the long bones, which can splinter and poten-tially cause serious problems. You can give your cat turkey or liver or chicken parts; the "heinie," the liver, heart, gizzard, and muscle meat are all perfectly fine. You don't even have to worry about the fat content.

Will Cats Eat Their Veggies?

Although I have never come across a vegan cat, there are animals that enjoy vegetables. Good, you can feed vegetables to them—unless it causes diarrhea. And believe me, you'll find out pretty quickly if it does.

Cat Tip: Some health-conscious people remove all the fat from their birds. This fat makes a great treat for your cat, unless it's overweight, as generally cats don't have problems with too much fat in their diet. Vascular diseases—in particular clogged arteries—is a human problem. Cats can tolerate a diet high in fat, so chicken skin, for example, is fine for them.

Is Cream Good for Cats?

A small percentage of cats are lactose intolerant, but most have no problem eating diary products. If you want to make sure dairy is healthy for your cat, give it a small amount of milk or cream as a test. If there is no diarrhea within twenty-four hours (did I mention that you'll find out pretty quickly?), then dairy is fine. A lot of cats love cheese too.

Should Cats Eat Eggs?

Eggs are an almost perfect food for cats. Eggs contain all of the amino acids—the building blocks of protein. But raw egg whites can be a problem as it can have an anti–vitamin B effect. But cooked eggs or raw yolk is a great, healthy treat if your cat enjoys it.

Do Cats Have a Sweet Tooth?

Most cats don't long for sweets, but some cats will eat ice cream. Cats generally don't do well with sugars, but a little bit of ice cream, *a little bit,* is perfectly acceptable — but only infrequently. On birthdays, for example.

Are Dental Treats Worth the Expense?

Recently some of the major pet food manufacturers have begun selling dental treats for cats. These are simply very large pieces of dry food designed to help prevent tartar from building up on the teeth. The Hills company, which makes The Science Diet, markets treats called T/d, which stands, I'm guessing, for treats-dental. The recommended three to five servings a day actually is a good treat and may help prevent tartar buildup. *May prevent.* Prevent is the operative word here, because if your cat already has a plaque buildup, this won't negate the need for dental cleaning.

What If My Cat Eats Everything?

Some cats will eat almost anything edible. Many of my clients tell me their cats crave melon or olives — and strangely some cats actually seem to get a little buzz from these treats. Many cats love butter.

Is Seafood Safe for Cats?

As I've mentioned, many cats are allergic to fish, so in general I would avoid it as a treat. Okay, here comes the *but*. But I have to admit that at The Cat Practice we sometimes have patients who refuse to eat or, more dangerously, won't drink. To compel them to take in the liquids they need, we bend the no-fish rule and offer them canned foods containing tuna and liver or mackerel and giz-zards. For those cats that need extra fluids, the water from a can of tuna packed in water can be extremely important. But, these are exceptions. Most of the time it's much better to avoid fish because those cats who are allergic to it may react by vomiting, develop-ing skin rashes, sometimes diarrhea and urinary tract problems. In other words, nothing good.

Do Cats Need Vitamins?

There are cats who love debittered brewer's yeast: Sprinkling some of it on their canned food will supply a good amount of many B vitamins. A few drops of wheat germ oil can supply vitamins E and A. But just a few drops because you can give your pet too much of vitamins E, A, D, and K, and the excess will *not* be excreted, but stored in fat and can create problems.

> **Cat Tip:** Butter is a great way to slip a pill to a recalcitrant cat. Just grind the pill into powder form and pick up the powder with a finger full of semi-melted butter. Most cats will happily lick the butter off your finger, but if not just rub it on their lips. Cats are fastidious, and they will almost immediately lick it off, enabling them to maintain their gloriously sleek and clean self-image.

Is Catnip Good for Cats?

For most cats catnip is a fine treat, particularly if your cat is a couch-kitty. The stimulant just might provide some temporary activity.

What Do I Do When My Cat Refuses to Eat?

If your cat sneers at the food you offer, don't force it to eat it. Don't make it a choice between that food or starvation. And if your pet isn't eating, do as we do at the Practice: Buy some Jr. Meat Baby Food—

chicken, turkey, beef, or lamb. We often use these small jars to finger-feed sick cats or cats who just don't want to eat.

Do Cats Eat Bugs?

It is not at all unusual for cats to eat insects. In the wild, cats will supplement their diet of normal prey with all types of insects when they are hungry. Which, with most cats, is *all the time.* Cats will also eat reptiles, amphibians, and just about anything else that moves to survive. Oh, come on, it's not that awful, humans eat everything from chocolate-covered ants to fried grasshoppers.

cat tales: My great cat Renfield enjoyed flies, but he would also eat spiders, roaches, and just about anything else that slithered, crawled, or flew. Moths in particular were a treat, and we would often see a residue of moth-wing dust around his smiling mouth. The thing I found most distasteful with Renfield, and several other cats, was watching—and hearing the unmistakable crunch—as they ate a cockroach. Cats basically see cockroaches as edible toys, first they play with them, then they eat them.

Is Eating Bugs Bad for Cats?

While that may not be particularly enjoyable for you, I have never seen a single case of insect toxicosis—a cat poisoned by eating a bug. The biggest danger to an insect-eating cat is getting stung on their nose or paw by a bee or wasp, which hopefully will teach it to ignore them in the future. Oddly enough, while there are several different types of poisonous spiders on the east coast and I've even been sickened by a black widow spider bite, I've never treated an animal that has either been bitten by or eaten one of them. I've wondered if cats have some type of evolutionary knowledge about which bugs to stay away from.

Do Cats Eat Dirt?

It's not uncommon for a cat to eat dirt. Pica, as it's called, is the act of eating nonfood substances. That might describe eating dirt, pennies, rubber bands, or any other indigestible items. Believe it or not, there are humans who do this too. Although no one knows the cause for sure, it's generally

cat tales: I did treat a potentially serious case of toad intoxication once. My cat, Whiz, was the scourge of our frog population. One afternoon Whiz came up from the pond to show me the frog he'd caught and was eating. But before long he started gagging, drooling, and finally retching. I examined the partially eaten amphibian and discovered it was a toad. Some species of toad have toxic and hallucinogenic substances in their skin. In the tropics, for example, primitive tribes will lick the skin of these hallucinogenic toads as part of ritualistic ceremonies—apparently toad licking was popular in parts of Colorado in the 1980s—but, living in Connecticut, Whiz was just looking for a good meal.

I immediately flushed his irritated mouth with warm water and then gave him milk. I treated him as if he had been poisoned. Whatever was wrong, my objective was to get it out of his system as rapidly as possible. Fortunately, he recovered and, while he continued to enjoy frogs legs and others parts of the frog, he had learned to eschew toads.

believed that it is triggered by intestinal parasites, vitamin and/or mineral deficiencies, and metabolic disorders.

During my career I've removed a bewildering variety of objects—referred to as foreign bodies—from the stomach or intestines of patients. I saved these objects so I could create a display that I believed would be instructional for cat owners, but my wife wouldn't let me keep them—she didn't want to scare people. I believe her precise words were, "Are you out of your mind?"

Can Cats Swallow Anything?

Yes, a cat will eat what a cat wants to eat. Out of all of the cats I've treated for ingesting foreign objects, the big winner was a cat with 18 cents in her stomach: a dime, a nickel, and three pennies. While I understand that cats might ingest rubber bands and Q-tips while playing with them, the coins are strange because money is not easy to play with or pick up—even if you have a thumb—and those coins would not get hung up on the rear of the tongue and swallowed. No, apparently this was a cat trying to prove she could take her wealth with her.

> **Cat Tip:** Cats will eat almost anything they find on the ground, without regard to whether or not it's good for them. The best way to prevent that is simply to keep small objects off the floor.

cat tales: Once, a pleasant woman brought in her cat and informed me he had swallowed a 12-inch knitting needle. The cat was about 16 inches long so that sounded pretty dubious to me. When I asked why she thought that was the case she said, "I saw it. He was playing with it and just swallowed it."

Surrrrrrrre, I thought. But long ago I learned that if you're not going to listen to what your clients tell you, you shouldn't waste time taking a medical history. She said the 16-inch-long cat swallowed a 12-inch needle, why shouldn't I believe her? So I took X-rays.

This was no needle in a haystack—this was a needle in a cat. Its sharp end was in the esophagus, its blunt end was in the rear of the abdomen. "Well," I said. "We're not getting this out with tweezers."

I began the operation by opening the cat's abdomen and found that the knobbed end of the needle had pushed the cat's stomach from the front of the abdomen to the back end. I began trying to manipulate the stomach so I could open it safely and remove the needle when my anesthetic nurse said sharply, "He's waking up."

Not fun. I checked the anesthesia machine, his heart rate, and reflexes. It didn't make sense. There didn't seem to be any way he could be regaining consciousness. I went back to my manipulation.

She shouted at me, "He's trying to lift his head!" Suddenly I realized what was going on. I held on to the knob of the needle and moved it slightly while looking at the cat's head. Whoops. It moved.

Oh, boy, I thought. The point of the needle was lodged in the neck muscles. The cat was still asleep, these movements were completely involuntary. That wasn't good news at all: It meant the point of the needle had penetrated the esophagus. Very slowly, very carefully, I removed the needle from the stomach and closed the small hole in the esophagus. Incredibly, the cat recovered relatively quickly and suffered no permanent damage.

cat tales: A few years later we admitted Benjamin, who couldn't stop vomiting, a sure sign that he had swallowed something. We did a series of Barium X-rays and discovered that he had a mid-intestinal foreign body obstruction. Again, I had to operate.

During the surgery I ran the bowel, technical talk meaning I palpated his entire intestinal tract. I found a hard lump in his small intestine, about halfway through. It was about as big as a medium-size olive. No problem. This was the same type of surgery I'd done countless times. Stuff gets caught in cat's intestines.

I gently clamped off the intestine a few inches on either side of the mass to minimize the contamination of the abdomen with intestinal contents and slowly began to cut the intestine to remove the object. Several members of my staff, including my anesthetic nurse, Vivian, were gathered around the table, staring intently, wondering what was causing the blockage.

I made my cut.

And suddenly a small green object with shining red lips and bright white teeth came flying out of the intestine. Vivian screamed and leaped backward, knocking over the surgical lamp. Instruments went flying. I stepped back involuntarily two steps, three steps. A couple of people literally ran out of the room.

The object landed on the floor and rolled a few inches, then stopped. It took a few seconds for the bedlam to end—and for us to realize we were looking at the head of a child's monster action figure. The cat had actually swallowed the head of a toy figure. We put the surgical lamp back in action and replaced all the instruments that had fallen to the floor with sterilized new ones and sewed up the animal. This certainly was the scariest surgery I'd ever done.

Why Do Cats Get Fat?

First, don't laugh. Cats have feelings too. But this is certainly one of the most common questions I am asked. Second, obesity in cats is not conducive to good health. There are certain medical conditions that can cause obesity in a cat, but unless your cat is diagnosed with one of those problems or suffers from achondroplastic dwarfism, a short-legged birth defect, it's probably overweight. Chubby. Hefty. Or, as someone once introduced their pet to me, "The round mound of love."

Why Do Cats Get Love Handles?

Those hanging love handles that remind you of a cow are the result of overeating. The fact is that people store their excess weight around their midriff, but cats store it in their inguinal fat pads located in the groin. The rest is gravity.

I've had overweight cats. I once had an overweight spayed female that we named, unfortunately, Bessie the Cow, because of her hanging . . . things. Okay, her hanging fat pads. So I know exactly what you mean. We'd watch Bessie the Cow waddling around and, admittedly, sometimes I toyed with the idea of tying an apron around her middle.

> **Cat Stat**
> Dry cat food is about 10 percent empty calories—also known as water—while canned food is as much as 75 percent water. For an average-size cat, generally between eight and ten pounds, approximately six ounces of canned food per day is a maintenance ration. In dry food that's about two-thirds of a cup divided into two servings a day.

How Can I Help My Fat Cat Slim Down?

You know you have a true fat cat: The question is what to do about it? Since cats have a well-known allergy to treadmills and Stairmasters, and few cats respond to 'Fetch, Tiger. C'mon Tiger, get up and go fetch it," exercise probably is not the answer. There are no diet pills or slenderella plans for cats. So the first place to start is food.

How Much Is Too Much Food?

The cause of weight problems in felines often is a diet *too* rich in dry foods. Dry foods are convenient—they don't have a strong aroma and stay somewhat fresh for a long period of time. The problem is complicated by the directions on many dry food boxes, which recommend three-quarters to a full cup per day for a nine- to ten-pound cat. For inactive cats, or those with a slow metabolic rate, this can be an excessive amount of food. For example, I once had a cat that gained a pound every four months on a strict half-cup-per-day diet.

cat tales: Renfield lived in a stable before deciding to bunk with my family. He was the poster cat for Dolly Parton's observation, "Once poor, always wanting, darling."

Nothing got between Renfield and a meal. While living at the stable he would try to steal food from a German shepherd guard dog who was so aggressive an assault rifle had been named after him. Renfield had never gotten enough to eat, so to supplement his meager diet he learned to catch flies, as well as eat absolutely anything he could catch. I didn't know this when I got him. He wasn't loving, or even attractive, but when I saw him back down a 1,200-pound horse in that stable I decided he was my kind of cat. That's when I let him adopt me.

Because he had been always scrambling for food, Renfield was lean and mean. But after a few weeks at my apartment, where he no longer had to battle other strays for food, he became big and mean, and then bigger and mean. He went from a welterweight to a light-heavyweight faster than I would have imagined possible. Finally I realized I had to do something about it.

Are Fat Cats Lazy?

Unfortunately, a lot of cats do grow fat because of laziness. Not their laziness, but rather their owner's. Too many owners just leave a bowl filled with dry food when they leave the house, or fill it whenever it's empty, or whenever their cat requests it. This can cause the cat to eat too frequently, not because it's hungry, but rather out of boredom or simply because they smelled the food. They eat a bit of it and go to sleep, only to wake up and eat again.

Is Being a Fat Cat Dangerous?

While fat may seem adorable, just as with human beings, being too fat can be dangerous. *The more obese a cat, the greater the risk of diabetes.* In addition, cats store fat in their liver, so when obese cats lose their appetite due to an illness, an accident or even just a disconcerting change in their environment, they run a serious risk of hepatic lipidosis—fatty changes in the liver that can be difficult to treat.

How Hard Is It For a Cat to Diet?

It isn't easy to put a cat on a diet. Think *Garfield* here. A cat has his whole day and night to focus on the one thing that really matters in life—the next meal. But don't worry, you matter too—because you're responsible for making sure your cat gets its next meal. The cat can ambush, harass, badger, plead, whine, scream, and otherwise demonstrate to convince its owner to serve him. Many of my clients have told me about one of the more irritating ploys used cleverly by cats to hint that they are hungry—standing on the sleeping owner's chest and breathing cat breath on their face while gently kneading their chest. This display of need is acceptable at 8 a.m. if the owner has to be up anyway, but too often this fish-breath wake-up call takes place at 6 a.m., or, as cats probably refer to it, "I'm hungry time." When one of my cats adopted this behavior the only thing I could do to stop it was to eliminate breakfast. I'd give him one-quarter of his food between 4 p.m. and 6 p.m. and the remaining three-quarters just before we all went to bed. No amount of plead . . . kneading caused me to change my mind.

How Do I Practice Tough Love with a Cat?

This is the first rule of leading your one-cat army: *If a cat is rewarded for waking up its owner by screeching, kneading, or trashing the apartment to get fed, that behavior will be reinforced.* The message is clear: *It works! Do it again!* Undesirable behavior should be met with an unpleasant response—a spritz from a water pistol or plant mister, being locked in the bathroom for an hour, and a resounding "No!" Corporal punishment is unwise and usually ineffective with cats. Remember, they're the ones with the sharp claws.

MEOW! **"There is no snooze button on a cat who wants breakfast."**

—Unknown

Can I Train My Cats the Way I Train My Kids?

Conversely, the same techniques that work with children will work with cats. Positive reinforcement works. On those blessed occasions when your cat does the right thing, either intentionally or accidentally, reward it with praise, stroking, food, or even catnip. For example, if your cat sits by the door screaming to be let out of the room, don't do it. Never give in, never surrender. But when the cat sits at the door waiting, praise it, stroke it, hand over the catnip, and open the door.

Does Neutering Your Cat Make It Fat?

Many cat owners believe neutering is the reason their cats has that hanging skin. That's not how it happened. Kittens require a lot of food to fuel their growth and activity levels. Most cats are altered between six and eight months of age, meaning they're not babies anymore. During this period a cat's rate of growth slows down substantially and its activity diminishes. Unfortunately, many times owners continue to feed their teenage cats with kitten frequencies and amounts, the result being a noticeable weight gain. Too often this is the first step on the path toward the fat farm. It's very difficult to overfeed a kitten, but very easy to stuff an adult cat. Cats older than six months should be fed an adult diet.

How Fat Is Really Fat?

The most obese cat I've ever treated looked suspiciously like a sumo wrestler. This cat led a cat's fantasy life: It was a deli cat and spent its day encamped directly under the meat-slicing machine. A rain of meat just appeared throughout the day. When it arrived at The Cat Practice in a cat carrier—truthfully I don't remember how it was carried in—I opened the carrier and was facing the first rectangular cat I'd ever seen. It was so fat it just filled the entire interior of the carrier. I finally managed to get it out and onto my scale to discover it weighed an amazing 12 kilos—26.4 pounds!

cat tales: I think Renfield was the first cat I tried to keep on a diet. He was agile and smarter than any cat I'd ever encountered. I put him on a carefully monitored diet and was shocked when I discovered he'd actually gained weight. I couldn't figure out how that happened—nobody bulks up on flies—until the day I was gardening in the front yard of my small Forest Hills, New York, apartment and found the grim remains of scores of pigeon beaks and feet.

When we lived in upstate Ithaca and Renfield could go outside once again, it proved impossible to keep him on a meaningful diet. Renfield was the greatest cat burglar who ever lived. I remember one time when my neighbor was barbecuing, or at least intending to barbecue, when Renfield literally stole a trail of linked sausages right off the Hibachi grill and was caught dragging them across the lawn.

The single most extraordinary theft I ever saw, however, was the day the phone rang just after I'd finished making myself a ham and cheese sandwich—I turned my back for a few seconds and when I got back and took a bite out of my sandwich I discovered the ham was gone. Gone. Renfield had swallowed the evidence, but neglected to wipe the telltale mayo off his whiskers. But it was remarkable, stealing the ham without disturbing the bread.

Renfield and I were in a battle. The weight-loss regimen was the standard method of decreasing calories. I certainly didn't go by the manufacturer's recommendation, which I believed was too high. I settled on one-third of a cup of good-quality light dry food twice a day. After a month Renfield hadn't lost any weight. I reduced it to one-quarter cup twice a day, still no loss. No loss? The less food I gave him the more weight he gained. Curious to discover his weight-gain secret, I spied on him with my binoculars and watched him successfully and successively beg meals from two of my neighbors. The older woman who lived two houses away told me she thought he was a starving stray. I pointed out that Renfield weighed more than she did—but she remained unconvinced.

But there was a consequence—when Renfield was eight years old he developed diabetes and I had to give him two shots of insulin a day for ten years. It was a lot of work and severely restricted our travel, but he lived to be eighteen years old and died of an unrelated stroke.

Can I Kill My Cat with Food?

Bottom line: You can kill your cat with love by giving it too much food. No matter how much it begs, restrict its diet. Use behavior-modification techniques—reward positive behavior and punish negative behavior—to train your cat to accept a healthy diet.

Can Cats Become Addicted to Catnip?

Catnip is not a drug. There is no such thing as a South American catnip lord. There is no underground catnip economy and it is not illegal. Many cats absolutely love it—but there seems to be an equal number who have no more interest in catnip than any cooking spice. Catnip is an international treat, enjoyed by cats around the world. It is, apparently, a natural part of their evolution. They may eat it, inhale it, roll in it, but I've never known a cat to try to smoke it. All cat owners have watched our cats get very excited or even seem to be possessed after a few nips. What is it about catnip that causes such a strong reaction? Well, first, certainly, is its scent. But the effects of catnip on a cat's brain and its behavior are not clearly understood—a nice way of saying we don't have the slightest idea. We do know that

> ## Cat Stat
> Catnip is a plant, *Nepeta cataria*. It is a member of the mint family. It grows all over the world and is known as catnip or, in some places, catmint. Believe me, it grows easily. If you have ever planted it, you know how it can take over your whole garden.

its effects are generally short-lived and are usually followed by a period of relaxation.

What's the Best Catnip?

Catnip comes in various degrees of quality. If it is available at a local farmer's market, fresh catnip is usually very good. Or, like me, you can easily grow your own supply. For dried catnip, at the Practice we generally use the product produced by Felix Company, which also makes a very good catnip-imbued scratching post. We have also seen our patients respond well to a brand named Cosmic.

Is Catnip Medicinal?

This herb can be used for several different purposes. We sometimes add a pinch of it to a meal to encourage sick cats to eat, which sometimes works and is a lot more pleasant than injecting valium or force-

cat tales: Because we use so much of it at The Cat Practice, I planted catmint in my garden at home several years ago. It is a nice ground cover with small blue flowers. But it very quickly took over and now attracts all the cats in the neighborhood—several of whom have long-standing feuds that have resulted in notched ears, nose scratches, and other battle scars. It turns out my garden on occasion becomes a gathering place where cats previously antagonistic gather to bask in the sun. I've seen my own cats resting blissfully with three other former enemies right in my catnip patch with nary a bad hiss between them.

feeding an animal. We use it out of necessity, and have found it to be particularly successful with cats that have slowly lost their appetite; in several instances it has proved to be life saving, as some cats suffer a form of anorexia that can prove fatal. In addition, catnip can be a very valuable training tool, used to reward laudable behavior like successfully using the litter box instead of the carpet.

MEOW! **"Essentially, you do not so much teach your cat as bribe him."**

—Lynn Hollyn

Can Cats Get Drunk?

I've never heard of a cat bellying up to the bar. Truthfully, in more than thirty years working exclusively with felines, this is something I've never encountered. I have heard about raucous rabbits getting

cat tales: Several years ago a young couple brought in a three-year-old altered male cat that appeared to be in very good physical condition. Its coat was glossy, its weight was normal, and there were no apparent problems with its musculature. Unfortunately, he was all messed up neurologically. He seemed disconnected to the world around him, staring, unresponsive, drooling, uncoordinated, and weak. His total repertoire of reactions was basically limited to lifting his head slightly at noxious stimuli. This was a very unusual situation, something I hadn't previously encountered.

I questioned this couple thoroughly about the history of this behavior with the questions I always ask: when it began, the presence of any toxic substances, prescription or recreational drugs in the house the cat might have gotten into. There was nothing like that in their house, so I eliminated the accidental ingestion of any of those things as the probable cause. Extensive blood tests, X-rays, EKGs, and a urine analysis also failed to provide any reasonable explanation for this stupor. I'm rarely stumped, but in this situation I really was stumped.

The next day I tried a different approach, telling the couple, "Look, I'm not any kind of law-enforcement officer and frankly I don't care what you do at home, but I have to ask again because I'm clueless about what might be causing this problem."

They looked at each other for what seemed like minutes. Finally, she said, "I think he might have eaten an ounce of Jamaican weed."

Marijuana. The mystery was solved. If they had been candid at the very beginning, they would have saved a lot of money. The cat was stoned. Within another day or so it had recovered completely. I can only guess that to this cat the pot smelled like catnip—although it still seems hard to believe that he could have eaten that much pot. So let this serve as a warning: You probably don't have to lock up the Jim Beam or the box of Godiva chocolates—but you might think hard about securing a stash.

bombed on beer, but as far as I know, cats abstain from alcohol. This is obviously a very good thing for domestic cats, because their livers are not capable of dealing with alcohol (as well as many other things that humans, and dogs, can handle—including acetaminophen, streptomycin, and many other antibiotics and nonsteroidal anti-inflammatories.

Do Cats Crave Chocolate?

Cats seem to dislike chocolate. Now, chocolate intoxication is not unusual in dogs, and it can be very dangerous. But I've never seen this in cats.

Do Cats Hate Water?

As we say in the office, most domestic cats do have an "aversion to immersion." However, there are several breeds of cats that do like water. Generally it has much to do with heritage. Large cats that live in very hot areas and depend on water to survive seem to love it, while cats from colder climates stay away from it.

Why This "Aversion to Immersion"?

Your cat may hate water. It might well be vanity—a wet cat looks terrible and probably doesn't feel normal with its coat wetted down. It might also be the fact that cats prefer warmth to coolness, which is why they laze in sunbeams. Water might be too cold for their skin.

What Is an "Aqua Cat"?

Obviously some domestic cats, aqua cats, as we refer to them, seem to be attracted to water. This is probably due to some behavioral stimulus that took place when they were kittens. These are the cats that play with dripping faucets and will even stick their heads under running water. I have known cats who occasionally liked to jump into the shower.

Can Cats Drink Out of Their Paws?

Lapping up water is a complicated task for cats, so it doesn't surprise me that some cats have figured out how to scoop up water with their paw and put it in their mouth. Cats do have skin between their digits, so they can literally scoop up water in this "web" and get a drink. This "webbed" foot also helps them survive in water if they have to swim.

Can Cats Swim?

Yes, cats can swim. Once in the classic comic strip *B.C.*, the character Thor saw a clam walking on legs. He went screaming to tell everyone, "Clams got legs! Clams got legs!" To which the clam thought, "Now he must die." Well, cats can swim! Cats can swim! And you're perfectly safe with that knowledge. As with most mammalian quadrupeds, swimming is instinctive—making them quadrupets! When a cat hits the water, his head instinctively comes up above the water level and he begins to "run" in the water, propelling himself forward. Notice I wrote cats *can* swim, not cats *enjoy* swimming. It's a survival mechanism, not something most cats do for pleasure.

cat tales: Whiz liked to hang around the pond we have behind our house, although I came to believe it was much more because of the abundant and catchable amphibian population rather than an attraction to the water. Whiz used to like to wade into the water and jump aboard our canoe as we approached the shoreline, but this was probably his love for his friends being stronger than his fear of water. Once he did miss his timing and, quite insulted, had to swim to shore.

Several of my clients own pleasure boats that they use in the summer and often take their cats with them. The cats seem to enjoy the salt air, the spray, and the solid deck. The owners tell me that their cats rapidly develop good sea legs. Truthfully that doesn't surprise me. I know that cats are extremely athletic and adapt quite well to situations requiring good balance.

How Much Water Should Cats Drink?

Drinking water is a whole lot different than swimming in water. It is extremely important that you continually provide fresh drinking water for your cats. By fresh, I mean changing the water frequently as water does get stale after sitting for a while. If your municipal water tastes fine to you, then it will be fine for your cat. If it has a sulfurous scent or is too highly chlorinated for you, then feel free to share your bottled water with your cat.

Cat Tip: The more dry food a cat eats the more water it needs. So if your small friend is on a dry food diet, you really should change the drinking water frequently. Most cats prefer running water to standing water: Imagine yourself stranded in a forest without water. You would choose to drink from a running rocky stream rather than a standing pool, knowing it's probably fresher and cleaner. I suspect that's why some cats really enjoy drinking from a dripping faucet. There are kitty watering fountains available, including the Drinkwell. This features a small pump that creates a waterfall into a bowl and includes a filter and a reservoir. We recommend these for cats on a dry food diet and older cats with kidney or urinary tract problems. They're a good alternative to a dripping faucet. It's been our experience that cats adapt well to the fountain and will drink more water.

MEOW! "Way down deep we are all motivated by the same urges. Cats have the courage to live by them."

—Jim Davis

Chapter 8:

It's ONLY PHYSICAL

MEOW! **"Some people say man is the most dangerous animal on the planet. Obviously those people have never met an angry cat."**

—Lillian Johnson

Cats possess amazing physicality. Athletes of the first order, they can jump, run, climb, flip, even dance—and land on their feet every time. If you doubt it, just remember the last time you left an open can of tuna on a shelf you were sure your cat couldn't reach.

The Cat Olympics

- Furniture Hurdles
- Drapery Vaulting
- Floor Skating
- Long Puddle Jump
- High Shelf Jump
- "Socker"

- Counter Gymnastics
- Mouse Wrestling
- Shadow Boxing
- String Fencing
- Sleepathon

How High Can Cats Jump?

As high as they need to! This reminds me of the unfortunate story of the woman who confidently put her perfectly cooked Thanksgiving turkey on top of the refrigerator for safekeeping. *That's too high for the cat to jump,* she figured. That was long remembered by the family as the Thanksgiving they had macaroni and cheese. The truth is, if you were to put Michael Jordan, Jim Thorpe, or even legendary high-jumper Rafer Johnson up against an equivalent-size feline athlete the result would be pretty much a slam dunk—so to speak—for the cat!

Cat Stat

So with all these muscles, how high can a cat jump? Physiologists estimate that a cat the size of a man could easily make a standing vertical leap from a sidewalk into a third- or fourth-floor window. Every cat owner has seen his 10-inch-high pride and sometimes joy gracefully leap onto a 36-inch-high counter. Thus, cats could easily "play above the rim." We've marveled at the ability of the great basketball players to seemingly hover in the air, but compared to them, a cat would stay airborne long enough to require mid-air refueling.

Why Are Cats Such Great Athletes?

Cats—large and small, in the house or the wild—are blessed with a remarkable combination of light, strong bones and very efficient musculature. Their light bones create an animal built for speed and quickness. Their muscles are strong, but their greatest ability is the fine muscle control they have, which enables them to change direction before they run into that living room wall. They are able to race short distances at high speeds and still turn fast enough to follow a mouse. That's typical, we've all seen our cats leap through the air after a toy or rodent and seemingly change direction in mid-air. And if you've ever seen a serious cat fight you know that the fighters really do look like combatants in a cartoon—just a whirl of fur. On the

Cat Stat

There is a distinct physiological difference between your muscles and those of your cat. Feline muscles contain pain sensors, stretch sensors, and fine motor-control sensors. In fact, cats have seven times the number of muscle sensors of humans and are able to generate enormous pressure measured in pounds per square inch. The Great White shark is king of this category, but cats are in the top ten for their strength of their temporomandibular muscles—biting power—ability. People generally don't think of cats as being particularly strong animals, but that's because they sometimes forget the relationship between house cats and cats in the wild. Think of it this way: How well do you think the heavyweight champion of the world would do in a fair fight against a cat of equal weight? I rest my case.

other hand, if you see cats throwing left jabs and nipping at the neck or flank of their opponents, they're playing their version of the Golden Paws.

Why Don't Cats Go Bald?

Actually, cats do go bald—but unlike human beings they don't use bottles of hair-restoring tonics, and I've never been asked to do a hair transplant. And it doesn't seem to affect their self-esteem or social life. But sometimes what appears to be baldness can be a warning sign of a more serious problem.

There is a feline medical condition called Feline Endocrine Alopecia, which is simply medicalese for cat hormonal hair loss. So male pattern baldness and hormonal cat hair loss is a common problem—the difference is in the location.

Cats Lose Hair *Where*?

While for men it's generally on the top of the head, for cats it takes place on the underbelly; feline baldness affects the cat's groin area—the rearmost underbelly. Okay, the crotch. Baldness in men is infinitely more troublesome and obvious, and most men—with the obvious exception of exhibitionists—would probably trade their chrome dome for a pubic area fallout.

I just can't imagine a cat, as vain as we know they are, doing a crotch comb-over. In fact, they seem to be gloriously unabashed about it. Several times each month clients will bring in their cats, worried about this inguinal hair loss. I ask if they have seen their cat over grooming that area? Almost invariably they confirm that that is exactly what's been happening. There isn't too much we can do to stop this behavior, cats spend a significant amount of time working on this area. For cats it's important to keep this area clean, so sometimes what my client takes to be over grooming is actually normal cat behavior.

Cat Tip: Before calling the vet, or the cat hairdresser, take a look at your cat. If the hair loss is accompanied by reddening of the skin erythema, macules, and papules—hives—or erosions and ulcers, then we're dealing with skin problems that will require treatment. There is an old saying about human dermatology, "No one dies and no one gets any better," the point being that many different skin problems manifest themselves with similar symptoms. Biopsies are often required to determine if we're dealing with a staph infection, a fungal problem, a virus, an allergy, psoriasis, or eczema.

When Is Grooming Too Much Grooming?

In situations where cats are losing their hair because of over grooming rather than cat pattern baldness, I usually find evidence of some hairs cut in half by the cat's sandpaper-like tongue. This is a separate problem caused by over grooming, but it can be symptomatic of other problems. When I see this I always look for anal gland problems or feline urinary tract syndrome (FUS). If, however, there are no butch-ered hairs, but rather bare smooth skin with no evidence of trauma, hives, or other skin lesions, then we're talking about the very benign problem of Feline Endocrine Alopecia!

Do Cats Get Ringworm?

I have seen cats that are bald on the top of their heads. Usually it's a symmetrical hair loss, sometimes marked by flakiness, occasionally mild redness—and it tends to spread. This is usually a symptom of ringworm, a poorly named fungal disease of the hair shaft or fol-licles. It's called ringworm because in people it can cause a raised red ring on the skin. Here's the biggest danger though: This usually mild, self-limiting fungal skin disease is contagious between pets and their owners. Some animals can carry this disease and have no overt symptoms, which means you might pet a friendly dog in the park, then come home and pat your cat—the result being another visit to the vet for Feline Baldness.

Ringworm isn't some-thing you should worry about. Both animals and their owners eventually will develop immunity to ringworm, especially if the human component has

cat tales: Several years ago a friend had a tame and highly amusing crow named Jim. This Jim and I became friendly, and several days later I developed a ringworm problem. Only then did I learn that birds apparently have a different form of this fungal disease, a form to which I obviously had not yet developed an immunity.

had several pets when they were younger. Most people have probably already had a case of ringworm that they don't remember or didn't even recognize in the form of a mild subclinical disease. I handle cats with ringworm all the time and never have a problem. Well, at least not with common cat and dog ringworms.

Do Cats Sweat?

On the sweat scale, cats are not as naturally cool as elephants but are much cooler than mice. And like many living things, they sweat. Cats have very efficient thermoregulatory skills. Even in many extreme conditions, they are able to maintain their core temperature within their normal temperature zone, 100.5 to 102.5. To do so, they employ the same tricks as other mammals. For example, when you

see a cat shivering, he is simply increasing muscle activity to generate warmth to ward off the chill.

Cats *lower* their temperature by sweating. But cats, with their gorgeous, all-natural fur coats do not have exposed skin, so they lack the tools to cool themselves this way. To survive, they had to come up with something quite different.

Unlike us hairless, upright mammals, cats have a limited number of sweat glands, which are found mainly in their foot and toe pads. I often see little wet tracks on my examining table as my patients sweat out their anxiety-based pseudo-fevers. So yes, cats sweat, but they will never let you see it. They'll be no beads of sweat running down their furrowed brows. Panting—mouth wide open, tongue lolling out—is very common among dogs, although not quite as frequent in cats. It's actually relatively rare.

cat tales: You won't often *see* a cat sweat. Cats just don't like to expose fear openly. The first time I saw a cat pant was in 1969 in Vietnam. My Marine battalion was moving to a new base and my men and my cat, Nguyen thi Meo, were traveling by truck on an extremely hot day. The temperature was about 115 degrees Fahrenheit, literally, and the humidity made it feel even more oppressive. Nguyen began to pant and I was so alarmed that I had them stop the truck. At this point I was not a vet, just a simple First Lieutenant, and I was scared for my cat. We put the cat in the shade and wet her down with water from our canteens. The cat was absolutely fine. So if your animal starts to pant, while it may seem a like respiratory crisis, it's almost always a response to high body or ambient temperature caused by the environment or anxiety.

cat tales: While you will rarely see a cat sweat or pant, you will often see young vets sweating profusely. At the end of our studies at the Cornell Vet School we take the New York State Veterinary Board exams. This test is a combination of written responses and hands-on examinations, and it lasts almost a week. For a lot of students, including myself, it is the culmination of a long dream and many years hard work—and is the only hurdle left between being a student and becoming a vet. So, things get a bit tense. Actually, they get a lot tense.

Manning one of the practical—hands-on—stations was a dour looking vet examiner, wearing plaid pants and a very hostile look. In front of him was an anesthetized beagle, and my task was to palpate his abdomen under the glare of this silent vet. I was sweating, long rivulets of sweat ran from my brow along my nose down my chin. It seemed like even my eyes were sweating—and every bead of it was dripping onto this sleeping dog. Finally, this vet looked at me and said evenly, "Young man, if you don't calm down, you're going to drown this dog."

Then, he smiled, making me feel a lot better.

Why Does My Cat Hate the Vet?

Unfortunately for vets, cats can become very uncomfortable outside their normal environment so a visit to the vet can be extremely stressful. They are suddenly and unexpectedly stuffed into a carrier—basically a prison cell—and brought through a noisy city, often on the subway, sometimes in a car, into an environment with a cornucopia of new scents. Some of my patients are terrified when they finally get here, which is magnified by the fact that they may not be feeling very well to start with. So by the time I see them, no kind words or soft strokes can allay their fears. They have become a pool of quaking feline anxiety.

This excitement, which results in those muscle tremors, actually can elevate their body temperature an additional 2 degrees. When examining very scared cats I often get a rectal temperature in the 103-degree range, even occasionally 104 degrees. I've seen this often enough not to be overly concerned about it, and generally within two hours the cat has adjusted to its stress and its temperature has dropped into the normal range.

Why Do Cats Drool?

Cats drool for a lot of reasons: For example, some very affectionate cats will purr and drool as they luxuriate in head patting or brushing. I've known cats who drooled at the whir of a can opener. Cats will savor pleasure and relax and often won't even be aware they are drooling. Not that it makes any difference to them—those aren't their shoes or their carpet.

Actually drooling isn't abnormal or even that unusual, although a lot of cat owners find it disconcerting—particularly if they happen to be sitting on your chest when they start drooling. And contrary to a common belief, drooling is not a symptom of rabies. Perfectly healthy cats drool happily.

Second, in addition to drooling for pleasurable reasons, cats will also drool when they're frightened. Drooling is a hallmark of fraidycats. Going to the vet, for example, is the cat version of a trip to the dentist. In an anxiety-provoking situation, like a medical visit, the drool will often hang in long strands from the cat's chin all the way—in my case—to the examination table. That too is very normal and is not a cause for concern.

When Is Drool Too Much Drool?

If your cat is neither ecstatic nor frightened and drools persistently, you should bring it to your vet. There can be several causes for this behavior, and it indicates a bit of distress. By far the most common thing I find when examining a drooling cat are bad teeth and a gum infection—usually involving the rearmost upper premolars. Unlike humans, whose main salivary duct empties behind the lower incisors, a cat's main duct empties on the

cat tales: I once had a cat we called GW. That did not stand for George Washington: It stood for Great White, a name he had earned. This cat had a shark-like eating behavior and he did so in a feline feeding frenzy. GW was the only cat I've known who almost had a seizure watching a can of cat food spinning under the can opener. Also, he drooled. I mean, he really drooled. Not just a fine dew around his muzzle, I mean torrents of saliva ran from the corners. I mean this was the Mississippi River of droolers. Fortunately, he wasn't particularly interested in people food and he disliked dry food but it took two people to open a can of Friskies—one to feed him, one to mop the floor.

outside of the last pair of upper premolars. Thus, people rarely see the buildup of tartar, which can lead to gum disease, inflammation, and infection.

Anything that causes irritation in the mouth can lead to drooling: This includes tonsillitis, pharyngitis, benign and malignant tumors, abscesses and foreign bodies. During examination I've found irritating plant stems stuck between teeth, small bones, and even sewing needles stuck in the hard palate. Plants in particular can be harmful to a house cat. The leaves of several different plants, among them Dieffenbachia (Dumb Cane) contain irritating chemicals that can cause mouth sensitivity and drooling if a cat nibbles them.

Finally, catnip will make many cats slobber. This is perfectly normal and your cat is not having a drug reaction.

Probably the most important thing you can do if your cat drools is make sure your expensive shoes are high off the ground. But drooling itself isn't going to hurt the cat at all.

Does My Cat Really Need Dental Work?

Many cats do need to have their teeth cleaned, although the frequency can vary. It might be every year, or it might be every ten years. Purebred cats seem to have more dental problems than other cats.

MEOW! "Everything I know I learned from my cat: When you're hungry, eat. When you're tired, nap in a sunbeam. When you go to the vet's, pee on your owner."

—Gary Smith

Chapter 9:

Friends FOR LIFe

MEOW! **"A cat improves the garden wall in sunshine, and the hearth in foul weather."**

— Judith Merkle Riley

When you have a cat as a friend, you have a friend for life. As with all friends, feline, human, or otherwise, you may not always understand or even appreciate your friend as well as you might. Like it or not, you may be influenced for better or worse by this association.

Living in such close quarters with a cat may put you at risk for a number of conditions, among them affinities and aversions such as the following:

Affinities for:
>Long naps
>Sunning in the garden
>Cream
>Grooming rituals
>Silk pillows

Pursuit and capture

Climbing trees

Purring when pleased

Scratching when displeased

Sleeping whenever possible

Independence

Aversions to:

Dogs

Rain

Cold beds

Hot stoves

Confinement

Confinement

Confinement

MEOW! **"God made the cat in order that humankind might have the pleasure of caressing the tiger."**

—Fernand Mery

Can My Cat Make Me Sick?

Fortunately, the number of diseases a human being can catch from a cat is very small. And that includes even minor illnesses. If your cat is an indoor pet and well cared for, your risk of catching anything at all is greatly reduced. And realistically, the odds of contracting something from a four-legged friend are insignificant compared to the risk of picking up something serious from a two-legged stranger.

Do Cats Get Rabies?

The most serious risk is also the best known: rabies. Cats are not natural reservoirs for this potentially deadly virus, but like humans they can be bitten and infected by a variety of small animals including skunks, bats, raccoons, and members of the canine genus. Regular rabies inoculations for your cat will all but eliminate this risk, which is why most states require this vaccination. Again, if your cat is a house cat the risk of exposure to rabies is not quite nonexistent, but it's very small.

Does My Indoor Cat Need a Rabies Shot?

I know how easy it is to let your pet fall behind in its rabies shots. Let me scare you: In some areas the local health agencies can mandate the confiscation, euthanasia, and brain analysis of your cat if it comes to their attention that your pet has bitten someone and is not up to date on rabies vaccination. Most of my clients assure me, "Oh, that isn't going to happen. Flipper has never bitten anyone." I listen, I nod, I sort of smile, and then I shake my head—because any animal will bite if provoked, hurt, startled, or scared. That's their first line of defense. Now, how does the Board of Health get notified when your neighbor's terrible two-year-old grabs your cat's tail and the cat snaps back? People go to a doctor or to an emergency room and these medical professionals are required to report all animal bite wounds. Then the animal's vet is required to document that the animal is current on its rabies vaccines.

Is It True Cat Poop Is Dangerous?

Toxoplasmosis is an organism that cats can carry. The animal may or may not show signs of this disease, but they do serve as a reservoir. Humans contract this disease partially through undercooked or raw meat and partially from exposure to infected cat feces. The disease can affect many different organs in cats and people—the brain, the respiratory system, and most organs. For this reason the disease is called The Guest Masquerader, because its symptoms can be nearly anything imaginable from anorexia to zygomatic swelling.

Cat Stat

All veterinarians are concerned with keeping our patients up to date on their vaccinations. We're their first target: Believe me, every time I stick my finger down a cat's throat I'm hoping that animal is up to date. During my examination I often evoke an unintentional pain response, which does lead to biting even in the most mild-mannered animals. Vets are also asked to deal with feral animals. Believe me, rabies is a serious concern to most practicing vets.

Should Pregnant Women Clean Litter Boxes?

Toxoplasmosis is of particular concern to pregnant women because if they are infected, especially during their first trimester, their babies can be born with significant birth defects. This isn't very common, but it does result in enormous legal awards against obstetricians. This is one of the primary reasons many baby doctors strongly recommend that a pregnant woman be tested for this disease—or get rid of her cat. Obviously there are some alternatives to the latter approach. Your vet can test your cats for the presence of toxoplasmosis titres. Unfortunately, the results of this test can be confusing to interpret; however, if both of the antibodies for which the cat is tested are not present the cat is safe.

But probably the best precaution for a pregnant woman to take is to stay far away from the litter box—even if the cats have tested negative. For the duration of the pregnancy, litter box duty belongs to the husband. That is the least he can do.

Can I Get a Fever from a Cat Scratch?

Bartinella—aka the organism that causes cat-scratch fever—is a bacterium which can infect a cat's mouth and upper respiratory system. It can be transferred to humans by biting or scratching—which is where its common name, cat-scratch fever, comes from. It can produce a fever, local redness, and swelling and enlargement of the lymph nodes. Fortunately, for me, this is a pretty rare disease. Otherwise I would have gotten it many times, having been bitten or scratched countless times over thirty years. There are some symptoms you can look for: Many infected cats have very extremely reddened gums. Dental tartar can also cause a reddening, but it is usually found around the tartar accumulation. A more diffuse inflammation, with little tartar present, is characteristic of the presence of bartinella. There is a simple blood test that your vet can use to test for this bacterial infection, and it's very treatable with a special antibiotic, Azithromycin. This attention to your cat can further reduce your chances of infection.

Can You Catch Parasites from Cats?

Visceral larval migrans is a very formal name for the abnormal infection and migration to humans of a cat's intestinal parasites. This is most commonly transferred to toddlers who come in contact with cat or dog feces that have contaminated their play areas. Okay, it's disgusting, I know that, but many toddlers seem to check things out by touching and tasting. Frequent analysis of your cat's stool by your vet can pretty much eliminate this risk. Outdoor pets should be checked frequently for parasites, especially if there are young children in the house. It's not something to worry about, as it's rare, but it is something to know about.

Can My Cat Give Me Diarrhea?

Giardia lambia is a protozoan contaminant of feces that produces diarrhea in man and beast. You can catch this from your cat, but it's much more likely you'll get it from eating at a deli salad bar. In New York City we often refer to these ubiquitous deli salad bars as Giardia bars. Your cat can easily be tested for this and treated, especially if the symptom is persistent diarrhea. Actually, this is one of those illnesses that *you* can pass to your *cat*.

What about Fleas, Mites, and the Like?

With the exception of those parasites I've already mentioned, most of the parasites carried by cats are very little risk to people. You can get bitten by your cat's fleas, but they would probably rather stay in their nice comfortable furry home than leave for your parts. You can't get ear mites. Tapeworms are generally species-specific as are most parasites. And the exceptions don't occur often enough for you to worry about them.

Can My Cat Give Me Cancer?

There is absolutely no link between any cat cancers and people. Several decades ago, irresponsible scientists published a paper hinting at a link between the feline leukemia virus and leukemia as it occurs in people. As a result of this, some cats were euthanized. There just is no connection at all, so this is something you just don't have to be concerned about.

Can I Catch the Flu from My Cat?

The dreaded flu is a viral disease and we do know that influenza viruses can mutate and cross species boundaries. Examples of this are the swine flu and, more recently, the avian flu or bird virus. So it's not outside the realm of possibilities that a mutated feline virus could sicken humans and, conversely, that your flu virus could attack your precious feline. However, as of yet there is still no proof that this has ever happened.

Can I Train My Cat to Travel Well?

There are a few things you can do to make traveling a little more pleasant for your cat, especially if you get the cat as a kitten. Everything is new for a kitten so very early on take them on short trips. Always keep them in their carriers but continue talking to them and stroking them. You might even give them a treat. By gradually making these trips longer and longer, you may well end up with a cat that travels easily.

cat tales: This is something I've paid attention to, out of curiosity, and I've noticed that often when a house cat has some vague viral signs it isn't at all unusual that someone living in that house has recently been ill with flulike symptoms. We know that cold viruses mutate easily. Could these viruses cross the species boundary? It seems possible—but it's far more likely people caught that cold from a doorknob, from being in a crowd in the supermarket, or from a relative.

The reality is that I spend most of my workday kissing cats, getting scratched, contaminated by urine and feces—and I've only missed six days due to illness in thirty years. And never, as far as I can determine, from anything related to working with cats. So don't worry about getting any disease from your cat—and go ahead and give it a big kiss!

Do I Have to Use a Cat Carrier?

Let me emphasize that small animals of any kind should never be permitted to roam or rest free in a car. In the event of an accident, the animal becomes a furry missile, posing a serious danger to both the animal and the occupants of the car. Another risk, particularly with cats who like to explore, is that the cat may end up in the driver's footwell or even under the brake pedal.

Can My Cat Fly?

Cats can fly, but it does require preparation. Air travel can be very scary for cats. It's generally a series of new and loud events and because the cat is confined it can't do what ten thousand years of experience have taught them—run! An airplane trip starts with a challenging drive to the airport. Then there is usually a long wait, during which time the cat will be exposed to thousands of new and confusing scents, which generally will put the cat into a nervous frenzy.

cat tales: Good old Renfield hated being confined in his carrier, so I thought he might calm down if I let him out of it. In fear, he went into his hiding mode and found the safest place to be—directly under the brake pedal. Trust me, driving sixty miles an hour without the use of my brakes was not a good thing. Luckily I was able to coast off the highway and stop by putting on my emergency brake. I then was able to get Rennie back in his carrier.

Amazingly, all that happened while Renfield was tranquilized. Remember, your vet can give you mild and safe tranquilizers for a trip—but nothing can turn your cat into a rug. The effects of any tranquilizer can be reduced if the cat releases enough adrenaline.

Again, there are some things you can do to reduce stress. First of all, no matter where you're going, make sure the carrier is comfortable. You might want to cover the floor with something soft and familiar, a well-used undergarment will provide the reassurance of your own familiar smell. Also, it's probably a good idea to sprinkle catnip liberally in the carrier to overwhelm most of the other scary odors.

Cat Tip: Here's the best approach to traveling with your cat: Don't! Unless you are going on a prolonged trip, consider leaving your cat home. Your cat will miss you, but maybe not as much as you hope. And surrounded by familiar family, friends, or even reputable catsitters, it will survive quite happily. If that isn't possible, consider boarding your cat, especially if you can find a place locally staffed by cat lovers, reassuring supervisors, and cat toys—The Cat Practice, for example.

Boarding your cat with your vet is a good way for the cat to have its annual examination and get all the necessary shots while in a safe, reassuring environment.

How Does My Cat Know We're Going to the Vet?

As I've written, it's highly unlikely your cat is psychic. But it can sense changes in the environment. Generally when asked this question, I can't resist looking the person right in the eye and asking seriously, "Was the cat in the room when you made the appointment?" Admittedly, they often don't find this question as funny as I do.

Actually, preparations for the trip to the vet can make a cat owner nervous, which causes them to produce a fear scent that animals will pick up; they won't recognize the going-to-the-vet smell, but just an unusual anxiety, enough to alert them that something is wrong and they'd better find someplace to hide until they can figure out exactly what the problem is.

How Do I Get My Cat Into the Carrier?

Once the carrier is in plain sight, you've lost the element of surprise. Game over. Your cat, being smarter than every other cat, will find the safest place to hide in your home. "Safest" in this instance meaning that place that you can't get to no matter what you do. Practically every day my receptionist gets a call from an angry, upset, or frustrated person explaining, "I can't make my two o'clock appointment. I can't get my cat out from under the armoire."

Again, there are a few tricks you can try:

1. First, don't ever get the carrier out until the cat has been secured in a small area from which there is no escape.
2. Stay calm: This is a good time to do some yoga. If you don't know yoga, this would be a good time to learn.
3. Get your biggest and thickest bath towel and speak softly and soothingly, promising absolutely anything, and drop that towel over your bucket of love. Wrap the cat up in the towel and stick the entire bundle into the carrier. If the towel with a cat wrapped in it won't fit in the carrier, ease the cat directly into the carrier.

Cat Tip: It really is very important that you prepare the carrier to reduce the stress overload in any way possible—catnip, a soft bottom, a DVD player. Carriers get bounced around, and if the bottom is hard the cat is going to be even more uncomfortable. Make certain that the carrier is large enough to enable the cat to turn around, but not so big he or she will rock and roll inside as you move. You can carry more than one cat in a carrier—sometimes the companionship will help—but make sure the carrier is sufficiently large enough for the cats to have enough space. Some cats prefer carriers that they can see out of, others like to feel safe in a somewhat dark, confined space. It's not necessary to decorate the carrier. And personally, I discourage I VISITED THE GRAND CANYON stickers on carriers.

Work with the vet to make the visit as easy as possible. Don't try to help if you're not asked to help. An experienced vet knows how to handle cats. I always give my patients catnip lollipops at the end of a visit. And when you return home, give your cat a big treat and make a fuss over him or her to try to get it back into its routine as quickly as possible.

Can I Take My Cat Abroad?

If you are going to be traveling out of the country, it is essential that you find out all the regulations long before you go. That means contacting the airline or cruise line as well as the authorities at your destination. Your cat may have to have shots, there may be an incubation period at your destination, you may run into regulations you never considered. Don't put this off.

Will My Cat Be Jealous of My Baby?

We've all heard the myth that jealous cats will steal a baby's breath by covering its mouth, or sleep on the baby's face and smother the child. The myth has even found its way into classic literature: In Joseph Heller's *Catch-22*, a character had nightmares that his cat was sleeping on his face and he would wake up screaming. Naturally, at the end of the book, the character is found dead, his cat asleep on his face.

The rationale behind the myth is that cats are attracted to a baby's milk breath and may unintentionally rest on the child's face. In reality, that's balderdash and hogwash. In general, cats act protectively toward kittens and babies. Think how an adult cat reacts to a kitten. After the initial introduction, which usually includes some hissing and avoidance—cats tend to be reactionary and don't like change—adult cats almost always treat kittens with parental gentleness. They often will allow kittens to eat first, and even protect them while they are eating. They'll play with the kittens by allowing them to chase their tails and won't object when kittens attack. They permit kittens to crawl all over them while they're sleeping and nip at their ears. Amazingly, they also extend this forbearance toward kittens to babies.

cat tales: Rather than being a danger to our children, whenever our babies cried the cats mobilized and headed straight for the nursery, where it appeared they were ready to stand guard. When my eldest daughter, Ali, began crawling, she actually made it all the way over to the sleeping Ajax, a stray who'd found me and took great pride in being one tough critter—and a bit of a loner. My wife had given him his fitting nickname, Short Fuse. Basically, he defined his personal space as, well, the entire world. He rarely hesitated to use his claws or teeth to maintain control. (Maybe he wasn't the best cat to keep in an environment with a curious baby.)

So there was Ali on direct path toward the sleeping Ajax. As I realized what was about to happen I leaped into action and . . . too late. Ali grabbed Ajax's tail in her fist. Ajax was startled awake and, apparently disturbed, with his claws retracted gently pushed her hand off his tail and walked out of the room. If an adult had grabbed his tail the result would have been a trip to the emergency room where the wounds would have to be stitched up. But somehow Ajax knew that the human grabbing his tail was not a threat and had no malicious intent. He treated Ali with the same gentleness he would have treated a kitten. This took place while I was in vet school and caused me to start my own little research project. I wanted to learn the history of the relationship between adult cats and baby humans. I scoured the records of several hospital emergency rooms as well as the CDC in Atlanta—and I could not find a single reference anywhere of a cat attacking or injuring a baby. *Nothing.*

And all these years later, I still have never come across an incident of a cat intentionally injuring a baby. Don't write: Please, I'm not naive. I'm sure there are stories about such incidents, but there are also stories of people cutting off the branch of a tree on which they are sitting. It's just not ordinary behavior—and by now I can firmly state an isolated incident is not typical of this relationship.

How Can I Prepare My Cat for My Baby's Arrival?

It certainly seems that these folk tales about cats in nurseries are totally without merit. Believe it or not, your cat may sense you're pregnant before you do. That knowledge gives them months to get used to the reality that the dynamics of the household are going to change. After the child's birth, there will be several more months before he or she begins crawling, giving the cat a long time in cat years to become adjusted to change.

I also believe it's very important to try to keep those things most important to your cat—meals, meals, and meals—as normal as possible. Try to feed your cat in the same place at the same times as before your child came into the house, and hard as it might be find time to scratch its head or make some other gesture of affection, these are important reminders to an animal that while there is a new addition to the environment it is not being pushed out or threatened.

But bottom line, I have never known a cat to intentionally injure a baby.

When Should I Put My Ailing Cat to Sleep?

This is the hardest decision a pet owner will ever have to make. It is agonizing. I know because I've had to deal with it at least once each week for the last thirty years—and on occasion with my own cats.

Most vets are in this profession because we love animals and have dedicated ourselves to preserving and protecting their life. Most vets I know share my belief that euthanasia is only appropriate when there is an irreversible fatal disease and a lack of quality of life. These two criteria are critical because we are the people who have to administer the fatal injection. Clients may be devastated,

cat tales: When I took my first job out of vet school with a small-animal practice in lower New York State, I didn't know when I accepted the job that the owner of the practice was also the county's Animal Control Officer. Unwanted cats and dogs ended up at our facility and, if unclaimed after sixty days, we had to euthanize them. My second day on the job I was told to go out back and euthanize the three dogs that had red tags on their cages.

What the hell is going on here? I wondered.

He described himself as "an animal Dr. Mengele." His words, not mine.

I refused to do this job, which precipitated an argument. I explained that I'd spent the better part of a decade studying so I could heal animals and I wasn't about to start my career by killing them. He sneered at me, "What are you, one of those bleeding-heart liberals?"

"No," I replied. "I'm actually a Marine with a Purple Heart from Vietnam." I was out of there in the proverbial New York minute.

but we're the people who bear the responsibility and have to deal with our own guilt.

I've actually had clients request that I euthanize their cat because they were moving to a no-pet building or because the cat was soiling the carpet or clawing the leather couch. I actually had the mother of a friend ask me to put her cat to sleep because he was clawing her valuable Persian carpet. Obviously I have nothing positive to say about people who have so little regard for the sanctity of life or the responsibility of pet ownership. To even conceive of ending a life for convenience sake or for decorating is beyond my understanding. It makes me believe there is something defective in their own life. These are the people for whom pet rocks were created. Unfortunately, I have to hold my anger and counsel them on the options that exist, but I absolutely refuse to euthanize except under the two conditions I've mentioned.

When Is the Right Time to Put Down a Terminally Ill Cat?

At times diagnosing a pet with a life-threatening disease can be difficult, and, unfortunately, expensive. Abdominal tumors, heart disease, and other rare, fatal maladies can require a broad workup. During this process, the vet and the pet owner need to work together to nail down the diagnosis and decide if treatment is a viable option.

It is a vet's responsibility to provide a quality of life for their patients using palliative medications or painkillers, but at some point we have to deal with reality. There are diseases that defy treatment. For example, pancreatic cancers and carcinomas of the mouth are often resistant to all forms of therapy and serve as examples of fatal, irreversible diseases. The question becomes, Is the minimal quality of life we are able to sustain worth it? It's an incredibly difficult question to answer. I've always believed that the people who live with the cat are best able to decide when the quality of life has declined to the point where we should consider ending it, but they need guidance from their vet in terms of what to look for. For example, most cat owners believe that their cat is in pain when it's yowling, but in fact, as I've explained, it's usually the opposite that's true. Cats in pain are usually silent and withdrawn. I've treated burned cats, cats with fractures, even a cat with a broken neck and invariably they are silent and withdrawn.

Why Is My Sick Cat in Hiding?

Cats in distress "go to ground." When animals in the wild, including cats, are seriously wounded or desperately ill, they will often crawl into a hidey hole for protection. Domesticated animals also change their normal behavior, they stop being social, they stop showing up for food or affection, they stay in a safe place behind the couch or in the rear of a closet. I get very concerned when an owner tells me the cat is not eating and is in hiding: I call it "going back into themselves."

Most of my clients faced with the "is it time?" decision are extremely stressed. They just don't know what to do. We begin by explaining to them the signs to look for, and almost always soon after they report noticing a definite change in the cat's behavior that signals its quality of life is slipping away. When a cat is brought in, I always carefully examine it before euthanasia and often find physical evidence that the cat is in critical shape. Symptoms include having a low body temperature, dehydration, and acting depressed and withdrawn.

Cat Tip: It is never an easy thing to end the life of a living creature, particularly one that has engendered such love, but sometimes the final loving gift we can give is to ensure that this part of our family doesn't suffer. When it is time, you and your vet can work together to provide a loving, peaceful end.

Should I Be There When My Cat Is Put Down?

There isn't a right or wrong answer about whether you should be present for the euthanasia, but here are some things I've learned through the years:

- If you are present, the vet is likely to take more time, be more careful, and offer you some support.
- If you are very emotional and demonstrative in your sadness, then your cat is likely to pick up on your emotion and may become agitated.
- If you are not present, it is perfectly acceptable for you to want to view the body after death. Some people simply need the closure. You may want to spend some time before or after saying good-bye. This is fine.

You must be prepared for your cat's involuntarily movements after death. The solutions we use are painless and usually work extremely

Cat Tip: As painful as it is, you should talk to your vet about what will happen to your cat's remains. New York City and probably most localities have rather strict requirements for the legal disposal of animal remains. It is usually limited to cremation or burial with a licensed animal mortuary. But you will have some options: If you have a place to bury your cat and it is permitted by local ordinances, your vet may be able to hold your pet's remains for a short time in his morgue—but generally not longer than a week. Remember, if it's winter and the ground is frozen, home burial can be very difficult.

Most localities do have animal mortuaries. These can be found in the local yellow pages or your vet should know how to contact them. In most localities this can be extremely expensive—especially when compared to cremation. But if you do elect to use a mortuary, ask your vet how long he has done business with this company and if he trusts them. There have been some distressing stories in recent years about unscrupulous animal mortuaries and crematoriums.

Most crematories offer two different choices: Group cremation in which the ashes are scattered on land or sea. This plan is usually half the cost of individual cremation in which you request the ashes of your animal. I'm fully aware that this is a distressing subject to think about, but it is important to be prepared so you don't have to second-guess your decision. Believe me, it can be very valuable to be knowledgeable and prepared beforehand when you're facing this extremely emotional situation.

fast, but they can cause muscle spasms after death. Touching or petting your recently deceased cat can cause its muscles to twitch and this can be very distressing if you're not prepared for it. A cat whose breathing is labored prior to euthanasia can often have spastic movements of the diaphragm for several seconds after brain activity and the heartbeat has ceased. Your pet's eyes will remain open after death no matter what you or your vet do. This is natural and normal.

MEOW! "I love cats because I love my home and after a while they become its visible soul."

—Jean Cocteau

Chapter 10:

The Nature
OF CATS

MEOW! **"You will always be lucky if you know how to make friends with strange cats."**

—Proverb

Cats are mysterious creatures;: Who knows what passions lurk in the hearts of cats? While we may never discern those darker feline emotions, we may very well imagine what might warm the cockles of a cat's heart.

For a cat, happiness is . . .

. . . a bowl of cream

. . . a pile of folded laundry

. . . a barn full of mice

. . . an empty bag

. . . a sunny windowsill

. . . a bed of catnip

. . . a climbing tree

. . . an open window

. . . a tethered dog

. . . a warm lap

MEOW! **"There are few things in life more heartwarming than to be welcomed by a cat."**

—Tay Hohoff

Why Does My Cat Sneer at Strangers?

Sit down and relax, your cat is not being judgmental. What he's doing is called *phlegmon*. He is simply trying to fully expose his vomeronasal organ—a small gland that is linked directly to the brain and is an important part in the whole breeding ritual.

Think perfume or cologne.

When females are in heat, males can smell their pheromones at a great distance, causing the vomeronasal organ—to send an emergency message to the brain ordering it to start the cascade of hormones that hopefully, if you're that male cat, will lead to mating. We know that a substantial portion of the feline brain is associated with the interpretation and response to odors. In predatory animals the ability to detect subtle odors is critical to their hunting and breeding needs. So they are not sneering, they are maximizing their olfactory senses.

Why Are Cats Obsessed with Bags?

This is another question I'm asked often by my clients. There is often some variation in the details, but the concern is always the same: What is my cat doing with this bag and is it dangerous?

Many cats like to lick plastic bags, although fortunately few of them actually chew on the plastic or digest it. Most of the time, it's

Cat Stat

What puzzles people is why neutered and altered cats continue to exhibit this breeding behavior. The answer is that although the testes or ovaries have been removed, these sexual organs are only the end point, so to speak, of sexual response. The nostrils, vomeronasal organ, and brain centers that are all part of the breeding system are still intact and functioning. So when cats sniff clothing or objects and then sneer, they are simply utilizing their vomeronasal organ to figure out what all these smells mean. They may catch a whiff of *eau d'cat* that came from a feline rubbing against the visitor's pant leg, or a dollop of dog drool that dropped on a shoe as the wearer scratched a dog's ear in the park. These are the kind of incidental encounters most people don't remember, but they carry the result with them for a long time. To a cat, an old shoe or even a fire hydrant can be of far more interest than Angelina Jolie.

nothing to be concerned about; small amounts of ingested plastic bags or wrappers don't seem to cause any serious problems. But that's only a small amount; obviously plastic will cause an intestinal obstruction if it is too large to pass through successfully.

Why the attraction? Well, that's easy to understand if the plastic has been used as a food wrapper. As far as a cat's scent is concerned, the food continues to exist on that plastic. But it's a lot harder to understand why a cat is noshing on or licking a dry-cleaning bag. Clearly there is a residue of something used in the manufacturing process that attracts cats. Supposedly animal fats are part of the processing of plastic, which might be the basis of the attraction.

Cat Tip: The best course is to keep plastic bags of any kind away from your animals—and if those bags have contained meat or other delectables that might appeal to your cat they should be disposed of in a sealed container. Don't leave temptation lying around your house!

Do Cats Have Supernatural Sight?

In more than thirty years of feline medicine this has happened to me at least two dozen times. After examining an animal I'll ask its owner, "How long has your cat been blind?" The owner will look surprised and then correct me, incorrectly, "No, no, my cat isn't blind."

Many cats go blind slowly and progressively because of retinal damage—and their owners just don't realize it. With cataracts people can easily see changes in a cat's eyes, and with acute blindness a cat's impairment is very obvious. But when loss of vision occurs slowly and over a prolonged period of time, it is not easily noticed—particularly if the cat has lived in the same environment for a long time. It's amazing how well blind cats maneuver in a familiar environment. Their coping skills are greatly aided by their other senses, particularly hearing and smell.

Cat Tip: Whatever the reason, it is very important to keep most wrappers of any kind out of your cat's environment. Some cats are very skillful garbage prospectors or dumpster divers, endowed with a seventh or eighth sense that alerts them when old food is available. The problem is that the string often used to wrap meats is permeated with beef or lamb juice and is thus perceived as a treat. If ingested, these strings can easily get caught on the forward-facing barbs at the back of a cat's throat or get stuck underneath its tongue or block the intestines.

If there is any chance that your cat has a string obstruction or any other intestinal obstruction your vet is going to want to take X-rays. The way most vets do that is to give the cat Barium and then take a sequence of X-rays until the barium reaches the large intestine. This can take anywhere from forty minutes to twelve hours. I'm pretty aggressive about using a Barium series to rule out intestinal obstructions. The Barium actually serves two purposes: It soothes the irritated intestinal tract lining, which buys me time for the medications to help arrest the cause of the vomiting.

Second, if a cat is obstructed, the bowel very quickly becomes inflamed, congested, and septic. It can begin to deteriorate within forty-eight hours, and can lead to an intestinal rupture with peritonitis if the surgery is delayed too long.

Cat Stat

For us, an apartment or even a house may seem still and static, but to a cat's supersensitive hearing that same place is alive with sound. It's roaring with traffic noise from outside, the whir of the refrigerator compressors, the ticking of clocks, the hum of fluorescent lights, the settling of the walls, and so many other sounds that we would never notice. But cats use these sounds to triangulate their position. Also, as blind people can utilize the tapping of their cane to get some idea of their location by identifying the echo, my experience leads me to believe that cats are able to use the echo of their clicking claws or meows to figure out where they are.

Can a Cat Smell Their Way Around?

I hate to tell you this, but your environment smells. Not necessarily good smells or bad smells, but easily recognizable scents. Cats smell as well as hear their way around. As discussed earlier, cats have a highly developed olfactory ability; to a cat a familiar environment provides a wealth of predictable odors—its litter box, the Lemon Pledge on the coffee table, various plants or flowers on windowsills, the ammonia under the sink, the roach motels in the hallway. These are all as bright as lights to a cat's brain to aid in navigation.

Why Do Cats Rub Themselves against Furniture?

Equally important is the fact that cats mark their territory with their own scent glands, which secrete chemicals called pheromones that you can't smell. They have these glands in their paws and on their cheeks between their eyes and ears where their fur is usually sparse. They have them on their lips and forehead. You often see cats kneading on objects—the purpose of which might be to sharpen their claws or mark an object or person. They also are known to run their cheeks or flanks against a leg of a chair or a human, even the corner of a wall. What they're doing is laying down "trail markers" to find their way around furniture or from room to room. They are creating an environment in which they feel safe and comfortable. When you've taken a shower or put on laundered clothes you've washed away these scents and they may need to be remarked, which is why your cat may rub against you or butt heads with you. Just as rats can learn and remember how to run a maze, it seems obvious that cats "memorize" certain important distances—the height of a couch or the number of steps up to the second floor.

Cat Stat

All of its senses come together to enable a cat without sight to find its way around a familiar environment. So moving an object in that environment, a chair, for example, creates a temporary problem for the cat. But after encountering that unexpected obstacle he will become more cautious until he is able to use all of his senses, hearing, smell, and vibration sensors and perhaps marking objects to put this information into its memory and relearn its environment. Cats are like modern warships, moving through an ocean of air with all its high-tech instrumentation pinging away to find its location and avoid any problems.

What Are Vibrissae?

Cats do have an additional sense that humans do not—even humans with long beards. It's called vibrissae and other animals share it. These are the small, sensitive hairs located on the muzzle that detect subtle vibrations. Sharks use these hairs to find prey and it seems likely these hairs evolved in cats for the same purpose. A cat's close-in vision is very limited. After a cat jumps on a mouse to immobilize it, for example, these small hairs help him locate the pinned prey so he can bite and hold it. As a cat walks toward a fixed object, a chair or a wall, he is literally pushing a small amount of air in front of him and these vibrissae can detect changes in the air current which serve to warn of proximity to that obstacle.

Do Cats Have A Sense of Humor?

A sense of humor is a pretty sophisticated concept for an animal who can find such great fulfillment in a torn sock. There certainly are a lot of jokes *about* cats, among them the well-known Tail of Two Kitties. It seems these two young cats were in love, and the tom says to his lady fair, "I would die for you." She looks at him skeptically and asks, "How many times?"

Can Cats Smile?

I do like to believe that at times I've seen cats smile, although mostly it's a look in their eyes. It's true, some cats have markings around their muzzles that make it appear as if they're smiling and when combined with the eye smile, I sometimes laugh out loud. But while cats might not be able to tell jokes or get involved in practical jokes, they do seem to enjoy playtime.

Are Cats Born Entertainers?

I have also seen many cats that truly seem to enjoy amusing and entertaining people. In human terms I would say this: They get the joke. In cat terms it probably would be more along the lines of, I'll do this for you if it gets me more food. For example: Another family cat, JG, once was lying on his back on the couch grooming himself when he accidentally slid off, causing my sister and me to burst into laughter. After that, on occasion, when both my sister and I were there, he would repeat this performance, knowing the result was going to be smiles, laughter, and some strokes.

cat tales: Growing up, my family always had cats. Until I left home for the University of Pennsylvania and then the University of the United States Marine Corps, there were always some aloof and fuzzy creatures around the house. Admittedly, not all of our pets were completely lovable. One, Red, as I named him because of his color, probably should have been named Attila the Cat. If he had a sense of humor it would have been very, very dark. His favorite activity—okay, joke—was to hide under the skirt of my Dad's favorite easy chair until my father sat down to relax with an after-work cocktail, took off his shoes, and leaned back . . . and pow! This cat would pounce, taking a nip out of my father's now defenseless feet.

"Geez!" My father would scream, leaping up and spilling his drink. Admittedly, it wasn't only old Red who thought this was pretty funny. But Red rarely stayed around to enjoy the joke, instead racing for safety behind the couch upstairs. I'd find him there, looking what I perceived to be completely innocent and unaware of the chaos he'd unleashed. And maybe even smiling.

Red liked to play with me, which is not unusual for domestic cats. My favorite was our foot races. I don't know how he taught me this game, but it started with my running around the outside of our house. I suspect I was probably encouraged by my exhausted mother, who wanted to tire me out. After watching me for a few minutes, Red would bait me to chase him. I was seven years old, so I still believed I could catch him if I just ran fast enough. Somehow he always managed to stay about four feet in front of me. Eventually we would actually run side-by-side. After a while, believe it or not, he would give me half-a-house head start. I'd take off in my new Keds, knowing that this time, this time I was finally going to beat him. Before I reached the first corner I'd glance back at him, usually to see him sitting contentedly on his haunches, licking his forepaws, seemingly unaware of the fact I was going to run him into the ground!

Usually I'd be in the lead until I passed the second corner—and then a red flash would zip past me, ears flattened by the wind. When I finally completed the circuit he'd be back at the starting line licking those damn forepaws.

That was Red's sense of humor.

What Makes a Cat Laugh?

Just like human beings, a cat's sense of humor has to do with its basic personality. More social cats will repeat behaviors that result in some form of engagement with other animals in the house or its human owners. Cats know, or at least sense, when they are receiving the attention they know they deserve. And you'd think that alone would make them smile.

True, there is absolutely no scientific evidence that cats understand humor, and logic would tell you that it is much too sophisticated a concept for them. But that has never stopped a cat lover—including myself—from believing that a happy cat smiles at us, and laughs with us.

Of course, from the cat's point of view, it may be that the joke is on us.

MEOW! **"I wish I could write as mysterious as a cat."**

—Edgar Allan Poe

inDex

Index

Index

ACKNOWLEDGMENTS

I would like to thank the wonderful patients and clients of The Cat Practice for their loyalty and kindness over the past thirty years. Also, special thanks to my wife, Ginger, and daughters, Alexis and Marian, for their understanding that some-times cats have to come first. Special thanks to my mentor, Dr. Paul Rowan, and my extremely capable associate, Dr. Victoria Sheheri.

—William "Skip" Sullivan

I would like to acknowledge those who have given me countless hours of pleasure: The Bomber, Beau, Catfish, and Buck. Most of all, I would like to acknowledge the support of my wonderful wife, Laura, who has given me so much love—as well as one badly clawed couch.

—David Fisher

ABOUT THE AUTHORS

Dr. Skip Sullivan completed his undergraduate studies at the University of Pennsylvania and then served in Vietnam with the Marine Corps where he was awarded a Bronze Star medal with a Combat V. He then attended the College of Veterinary Medicine at Cornell University where he concentrated on feline medicine. He has been tending solely to cats for the last thirty years.

Dr. Sullivan's veterinary office, The Cat Practice, is based in Manhattan. It was founded in 1972 with the purpose of providing our feline friends with the finest medical and surgical attention and their owners with the best possible communication.

David Fisher is the author of more than fifty books, including fifteen *New York Times* bestsellers. His novella, *Conversations with My Cat,* was awarded the *French Prix Litteraire 30 millions d'amis.*